Self Hypnosis

Tame Your Inner Dragons

Clinical and Psychic Use of Trance

by

Noel Eastwood

Copyright © 2016 Noel Eastwood All rights reserved

IMPORTANT LEGAL NOTICE

This book is intended to provide information to the practitioner and student of self hypnosis and meditation. It is stressed that the contents of this book are in no way a substitute for personal supervision by a qualified medical or psychological professional. It is recommended that you consult your health professional if you wish to compliment your treatment with meditation, self hypnosis or any of the techniques described herein. If you have an underlying psychological condition or are in crisis, please seek professional help. The author, editors and publishers accept no responsibility for outcomes if you use the techniques described in this book.

For privacy, names of individuals and parts of their experiences and identifying details have been changed.

This book is copyrighted. Apart from any fair use for the purposes of private study, research, criticism or review as permitted by the Copyright Act, no part may be reproduced without written permission of the author.

All communications to the author, Noel Eastwood.

Email: info@plutoscave.com

Website: www.plutoscave.com

Illustrator: Anthony Jones

Cover: Maureen McFarlane and Michael Eastwood

Editing: Kristal, Mark Eastwood

Table of Contents

Dedication

About this book

Dragons and our collective psyche

Introduction to psychotherapy and self hypnosis

Inner dragons - your journey to self

What is hypnosis and hypnotherapy

Tame your mind

Techniques, scripts and audio's

Inner space - healing

Children

Anxiety

Weight loss, smoking and relationships

Age regression

Sports hypnosis - mental rehearsals

Memory, study, creativity and dreaming

Psychic techniques

Past life therapy

Spiritualism, clairvoyance and automatic writing

EEG Biofeedback – Neurofeedback

The Inner dragon - my journey begins

Appendix 1 - Exploring the myths of hypnosis and clinical hypnotherapy

Appendix 2 - Common Psychological Defenses

Appendix 3 - About Noel Eastwood and Pluto's Cave

Dedication: *To my three beautiful children, Sonja, Michael and Steven: thank you for choosing me to be your father. Most of all to my wife, Marja, who gave me her love and the opportunity to realise my dreams.*

I would like to take this opportunity to thank my clients and students over the past 35 years who helped me grow to be the person I am today. To Harald Tietze, healer, dowser and wizard with a vision; Neville Andrews, my psychotherapy mentor who taught me not to fear walking my client's into the underworld; Chris Turner, astrologer, who taught me to read the individual through their archetypes; and Simon Lim, Taoist, who taught me the path to Tao. A very special thank you to Anthony Jones for his inspiring illustrations; Maureen and Michael for the cover artwork; my brother Mark and my editor Kristal, for kindly assisting in the editing and preparation of this book for publication.

ABOUT THIS BOOK

Parts of this book were previously published in 1995, as '*Maximise Your Mind: The Self Hypnosis Handbook*', it has since gone out of print. I decided to sit down and rewrite the entire book because so many amazing things have happened over the past 20 years. This is the result: a bigger, better and even more fascinating story of working in the unconscious for both the home meditator and the clinical professional.

This book aims to describe the many clinical and psychic uses of self hypnosis, meditation and the so-called trance state. The content and stories of this book come from my own personal experiences, students of tai chi, meditation, clinical hypnotherapy and psychotherapy.

The first half of this book is dedicated to the clinical use of trance and guided meditation. The second half describes how to develop your own psychic and spiritual potential using self hypnosis and specialised meditation techniques. This book is filled with true stories to illustrate these techniques.

I have drawn upon the impressive therapy of NeuroLinguistic Programming (NLP) to demonstrate how your mind communicates in a sensory language. By talking the language of the unconscious you bring to bear these modalities to experience your full potential.

I will not suggest that everyone that reads this book will be able to enter the self hypnotic or trance state easily. Achieving these results requires determination and discipline, 90% perspiration and 10% inspiration. If you don't put in the practice you simply won't get the results. I have spent the past 35 years studying the inner world of the unconscious and I am still learning.

DRAGONS AND OUR COLLECTIVE PSYCHE

Dragons have inhabited our culture since time began, these days they entertain us in the cinema and our lounge rooms. However tame and gentle we see them now dragons once represented a force of power and evil. Importantly for our own spiritual journey we can look to many fairy tales and legends containing dragons for hidden themes that can help illuminate the initiates path to enlightenment.

The story of 'St. George And The Dragon' from the 11th Century is a useful metaphor of the initiate conquering their inner dragon.

It is told that St. George travelled from England for many months across the seas to north Africa at the request of the Libyan King. A wicked dragon had made his home in a nearby lake and demanded a fair maiden for his daily meal otherwise he would destroy the kingdom. The Libyan King soon began to run out of fair maidens. All had been fed to the dragon except his beautiful daughter.

The Princess was on her way to the lake when St. George intercepted her. He faced the dragon and fiercely they fought until with great courage and the grace of God, St. George dispatched the dragon. Thus was saved the beautiful Princess and the kingdom of Libya.

Unless our dragons are conquered all that is innocent and beautiful all that has taken a lifetime to build may be ruined. The place where these dragons reside is our deep unconscious: an inner world that I call Pluto's Cave. Facing an inner dragon takes courage, strategy, dedicated practice and determination. St. George represents You in your struggle to overcome what is holding you back from freedom and happiness.

The dragon can be considered an aspect of our unconscious a manifestation of our repressed drives, urges and instincts. These instincts could be psychic fragments splintered from our childhood. Perhaps it is made of fragments of our psyche as the result of neglect or trauma or perhaps from a thwarted need for power and recognition. Whatever it is that we struggle to control can be representative of these inner dragons.

INTRODUCTION TO PSYCHOTHERAPY AND SELF HYPNOSIS

The human mind holds enormous potential to transport us through time and space even to places beyond our oxygen-rich atmosphere; backwards and forwards in time and deep within our unconscious to uncover memories long since forgotten. It can provide the answers to what appear to be unsolvable problems; enable your body to perform unbelievable acts of strength and endurance; it can trigger biochemical and neurological transformations to change us from charming peace-loving individuals into raving maniacs.

We know that minor changes in our environment can bring about profound personality change. For example, stress and trauma can trigger the release of nerve damaging toxins as does exposure to chemicals like dioxin and mercury; concussion and head injuries; shock, neglect, abuse, even a lack of sleep can transform our internal harmony. Our brain needs a healthy internal environment including good genes, balanced hormones, healthy biochemicals, proper nutrition, exercise and the 'feel good' of positive social interaction.

One small but important factor is the ability to bring an agitated mind into a calm and restful state. Self hypnosis, deep state relaxation and meditation are age old techniques that have the potential to bring about this desirable state of mind.

Throughout this book I have taken the liberty to use the term 'self hypnosis' to describe the process of all types of altered states of consciousness such as the trance state, meditation, deep state relaxation and the lucid state. You can basically substitute those words for 'self hypnosis' in most instances in this book. I have often used the terms 'trance state' or 'meditation' in place of self hypnosis to maintain the flow of dialogue.

If you are interested in experiencing psychic phenomena, then it is in this state that you will. For improved health, please try it. If you want to improve your sports performance, self hypnosis has been proven to help. If you wish to resolve the effects of trauma, this is a useful approach.

Through the dedicated practice of self hypnosis you can access levels of awareness only read about in books or seen at the cinema. You may eventually experience the freedom and sheer exhilaration of touching the limitless universe.

INNER DRAGONS - YOUR JOURNEY TO SELF

Dragons represent our unconscious urges, drives and instincts. We experience them as anger, fear, sadness, depression, greed, envy, frustration, competitiveness, love, passion, admiration, panic, criticism, dependency, selfishness, grief, grandiosity, worthlessness, hopelessness, helplessness and many other human emotions we may have suppressed. The term, 'dragon', is a useful metaphor that I use to descrIbe our unresolved emotions. It evokes useful imagery that can help us better understand what we are wrestling with in therapy.

We all use psychological defences to help us manage and prevent our dragons from reaching consciousness and upsetting our emotional stability. Defences do not free them from their prisons and it does not heal them. The result is that it binds the dragons to us like a ball and chain. I will discuss psychological defences later in this book.

Let me explain how I came to use the term *Inner Dragons*. Many years ago I worked with a client who experienced terrible headaches and struggled with insomnia. When he finally fell asleep he would often wake in fright with terrible nightmares.

At one of our sessions I guided him into a relaxed trance state, that special space where he felt himself floating out of his body through the doorway of the unconscious. He asked for and received insight into his sleep, nightmares and headache problems. When he returned to consciousness he told me he had the answer to his problem. It was all caused by a demon living inside his head.

This experience made me wonder: what sort of situation puts a demon inside someone's head? After considerable contemplation I decided that he should meet this demon.

My standard practice is to work with my client from their perspective. This is to avoid placing my own interpretation on what they are experiencing or to influence their thinking. He said that he hadn't tried to get in touch with his demon on his own but now wanted to try it.

At our next session I asked him to close his eyes and guided him into his inner world. He found his demon living inside his brain where the headaches originated. It didn't want to negotiate and it refused to release control.

I sent him home to continue his practice of self hypnosis and relaxation. I suggested that he might try to talk with this inner demon himself - if he wanted to. I knew that he would try anyway and I was also confident that he would be OK. I wouldn't let him do this if I had any concerns for his safety.

At our next session he brought a sketch he had drawn of the demon. He was quite artistic and his demon was pretty frightening. Over many sessions meeting and talking to the demon he eventually negotiated for it to back off and let him sleep. It did and slowly over time his headaches stopped as well. Although this process worked I never quite felt that this was the best way to deal with such an unusual phenomenon.

I then started to notice there were other people who had a similar 'demon' problem. I decided to find out exactly what these demons were. What psychological constellation did they represent? I had never heard of people that had demons living in their heads before and this was new and fascinated my inquiring mind.

The problem arose when I suggested to clients that they get in touch with their inner demons. That word DEMON conjured images of monsters and religious devils even of Satan. Many people balked at this raw term.

Then out of the blue, a client said:

"I can see the demon but it actually looks more like a dragon than a demon."

Ah ha! There was the description I had been looking for, it fitted this phenomenon perfectly.

It was my practice to direct people to create an inner sanctuary which is a special and safe place to go when practicing their self hypnosis. Some sanctuaries were gardens, a castle and by the beach or a river. They were all places where they could meet and nurture wounded, splintered elements of their psyche.

I would take clients into their past to rescue their inner selves and then to the sanctuary to heal and nurture. I decided that I could now introduce clients to their inner dragons while they were working in their sanctuary. This enabled clients to deal with their inner urges and drives while they also rescued their traumatised inner selves. It was an effective two-part process.

Sometimes when a client's personal boundaries had been severely breached by trauma, I would suggest they take their younger self to a castle. A castle was a very powerful metaphor for a safe and secure sanctuary for healing. It usually had a huge moat of water, huge walls and a cast of thousands of heavily armed, brave soldiers to protect them.

Introducing a dragon at the end of the garden, in the dungeons beneath or in the caves in the mountains beyond their castle became part of their therapy. It engaged a concept of wildness sparking a part of their psyche that was still unformed and unrestrained. It also put the dragon in a specific position of containment.

Clients enjoyed it too. Some dragons were destructive and had to be chained up in a dungeon: *"That's my mother from my childhood. She's going to destroy my sanctuary so I've put her in a dungeon to protect my vulnerable inner children."*

Some were reasonably safe but needed to be controlled and nurtured until they were ready to confront them: *"That's my brother when he went wild, he was cruel. I'm going to put him at the end of my garden. I'll put some soldiers to guard him. I think I'll ask the elves to visit and talk to him."*

Often many sessions of rescuing and healing past trauma's would pass before a client was ready to deal with their dragons. Some were relatively easy and plain fun. Often the dragon would ask of its own accord to be healed, to be rescued and tamed. Tame dragons were fun to ride and client's could explore much more of their kingdom than ever before.

These dragons became perfect metaphors for the unconscious urges and instincts that I had learned about at university. It fitted my model of the unconscious almost as if Freud and Jung had explained it themselves. It turned unconscious urges, instincts and drives into a form easier to work with.

From that moment onward, when special healing situations arose, I would suggest clients enter their sanctuary to find their inner dragon. Over time I found that there were many dragons inside us all not just one.

Dragons and unresolved early trauma

The more I guided my clients to discover their inner dragons the more I asked myself the big question: where do these dragons came from? I knew that many clients had experienced trauma in their childhood and teenage years so was there a connection to dragons here?

According to psychodynamic theory our inner selves (children, teenagers and adults) become separate or splintered parts of our psyche as the result of trauma. Trauma can arise from physical, sexual or emotional abuse, neglect, assault, rape, experiencing or witnessing domestic violence, psychological manipulation, dysfunctional parenting or physical injury to name a few.

When trauma occurs in our early years that memory breaks off and lodges in our unconscious. There it can become repressed hidden and forgotten but it never completely disappears. Trauma is often too toxic to remember so we develop psychological defences to keep them separated from our core Self. These defences serve to protect us from becoming overwhelmed, from being repeatedly re-traumatised.

These unresolved events in our life remain bad memories, memory fragments and repressed memories. They surface when triggered by external events such as a news item on TV, a smell, a song, the perpetrator themselves entering our lives or someone who may represent the perpetrator. There are many ways traumatic memories are triggered, even physical exhaustion can be a trigger.

Our psychological defences (also called Defence Mechanisms in Freudian psychology) attempt to protect us from these painful memories from consciousness.

Just imagine it as though there is a younger, wounded version of you who wants to become whole again - to be rescued. You may remember fragments because a memory is never completely suppressed or repressed. Psychotherapy aims to heal these traumatised memories and help you reclaim the energy used to suppress them.

I found that taking people backwards in time into their past using some of the techniques described in this book was a way to rescue these lonely, isolated and traumatised fragments of themselves. Those wounded selves could be adult, adolescent or a child. Their inner dragons fed on the fear of those lost and traumatised inner selves. By healing these wounded selves the dragons were disarmed and tamed.

I now knew why we have inner dragons. While clients continued to have unresolved issues from their past they would continue to have untameable dragons. They represented, in part, the drives, instincts and urges of psychodynamic psychotherapy.

Taming your inner dragons is ultimately part of your spiritual quest, the quest for freedom of the limitations placed upon you by difficult or traumatic life experiences. This book is also the story of how to combine two psychotherapeutic processes: rescuing traumatised inner selves and taming your inner dragons.

The magic of self hypnosis is that a therapeutic program (such as described in these pages) can easily be combined with it. Self hypnosis became the vehicle I used to introduce specifically designed programs and techniques for each client. Clients were empowered with their own individual program to use in the security of their own home and in their own time.

A story of demons and dragons

A client asked to see me to help reduce his anxiety. He came for therapy because I had helped his son manage his nightmares, and he trusted me. He told me that he couldn't sleep, was constantly on edge and he couldn't manage living any more. He was exhausted emotionally and spiritually. His wife told him that if he didn't get help she would leave him.

At his third session he told me that he had a demon living inside his brain. When it broke out it would attempt to kill any adversary, anyone who stood against him.

The client had once belonged to an infamous motorcycle gang and had done many ruthless, sometimes evil things as the gang enforcer. He had once been a very frightening and dangerous man. He had no fear, none, but he knew that life was more than the hatred he felt burning inside him.

One day he fell in love with a gentle, caring young woman. He knew that he wanted to share his life with her so he left his old life behind. They married and had two beautiful, gentle children.

He studied and worked hard to became a tradesman and never flinched from working 20 hour days when asked. Here too he feared no one and no task was too hard. However one day his inner world cracked open when he was attacked by a drug crazed man.

The man attacked him with a knife, he now found himself in a fight to the death. That is when his demon stepped in and held the crazed man to the ground. The demon punched his attacker until blood sprayed the gathering crowd. He felt such rage and hatred that he wanted to kill his assailant. Fortunately some bystanders stepped in and pulled him away.

After some discussion we decided to address the demon within his brain. I explained that we would start gently, taking him into his inner world to meet his 'emotional self' first. This is the part of his psyche that was crying out for help as it tried to cope with the madness building inside him. He built a sanctuary in that session and appeared reasonably relaxed

At his next session he told me that the sanctuary I had helped him create, which included his entire inner world, had been torn apart. Every living creature had been killed by his crazed inner self. Every blade of grass had been burned away and nothing lived.

I sat and thought for a while. This sort of violence in one's inner world doesn't happen very often - but there is always a reason. I didn't know what that reason was, yet.

I decided he should visit one of his inner children to stem this flow of rage, hatred and anger. But none were present. He had gone into every recess and every corner of his being and hunted them down. Then he killed them.

"They're weak, he hates them so he hunted them down and killed them," he explained.

At our next session we focused on the powerful force of his anger. It was then that he told me the story of his life and it all fell into place. I now knew what was happening in his inner world.

His grandfather was an evil man and instrumental in the mass murder of innocent civilians. This man viciously beat his own son, my client's father, every day. When this son had his own child, my client, he continued in the same vein. The father viciously beat and tortured his gentle little boy day after dreadful day. My client lived in absolute terror every minute of his childhood.

Then one day he stopped being afraid and faced his father without crying or cowering. He made the conscious decision that he would never be afraid of anything or anyone ever again. He then exorcised his 'childishness', his weaknesses. This decision enabled him to suffer his father's tortures without flinching. He became, from that moment, empty of all fear. He had succeeded in replacing his feelings of fear with hatred, loathing and rage.

In his mid teens he beat his father senseless then walked out. He left home to wreck fear and suffering upon anyone who stood in his way. At this point his demon had been released upon the world - and it liked it.

He told me that prior to the drug-crazed assault, this demon lurked just out of reach. He could sometimes see the demon in his dreams, in his nightmares. However he could now see the demon stalking him in his peripheral vision. It was time for a reckoning to stop it devastating his life, his family and his marriage.

For this confrontation I decided to prepare his unconscious by discussing demons as dragons. It was only a subtle change but that is sometimes all this process needs. The demon changed from pure evil to one that was rough, tough, powerful but open to negotiation.

By now his inner landscape was burned black. His raging inner self had torched the entire world and nothing survived. By the third week he had found two allies. A dingo (Australian wild dog) and a jaguar. They walked by his side in this dim and barren place that once was his sanctuary.

There in the dim light he challenged his dragon to come forth and face him. A shadow appeared and it crept towards him stealthily exuding pure evil. He was not afraid.

They sat down at a table together and negotiated a deal. The dragon agreed to back off and leave him alone until he was ready for their final confrontation. After many years service as his gang's enforcer he knew the rules. This was going to be a fight to the death and only one would survive.

They met for the final showdown at his next session. In his mind they sat opposite each other in a cafe. He was visibly tense to start with but then he relaxed and his breathing settled. I knew something profound had just happened.

When he came back from trance he told me that the dragon had transformed into a human and was dressed in a business suit. It said: *"Anger is as powerful as love but on a different dimension. You can use this power to change and I will help you. You now need me in a different guise to that which you have grown accustomed."*

It awakened something in him. His dragon had become his ally and no longer controlled him. Instead it advised him. He discovered that his barren inner world had now become a cityscape, busy and populated with people and activity of all descriptions.

He began to sleep better, his wife no longer threatened to leave him, his kids loved him even more. He began to feel something alien inside him. Was that love?

He came back from the edge to become the man that he was destined to be. Within a week he had left his dreary job and thus began his new life.

HYPNOSIS AND HYPNOTHERAPY

In the Classical Greek period healing miracles were associated with altered states of consciousness. The healing Temple of Asclepius at Epidaurus in Greece was used by sufferers to find the spiritual meaning behind their illnesses and other misfortunes. They prayed and offered gifts to the temple guardians. After two days and nights of fasting and supplication they were admitted into the temple for prophetic advice often in the form of dreams.

During the Middle Ages Kings were said to have the power to heal by the 'laying-on of hands'. Miracles were reported throughout history by great healers whose power was directly channeled through them from God.

Anton Mesmer (1734 - 1815) has been credited with being the founder of modern hypnosis. 'Mesmerism' and 'animal magnetism' are two terms we associate with Mesmer. In the late 18th century the Portuguese priest, Abbe' Jose' Custodio di Faria, was the first recorded to induce a hypnotic trance by using the words: *"I wish you to go to sleep"*.

In the early 19th century hypnosis developed quickly in many medical practices primarily due to the work of two doctors, James Braid and James Esdale. Braid described hypnosis as what we know it today: suggestions of sleep and the focus of attention. He was the first to offer the suggestion that hypnosis was not magic. Braid also adopted the word 'hypnosis' from the Greek word for sleep. He published his experiences in 1842 which incurred the skepticism of the orthodox medical profession.

Hypnosis was used by Braid and other surgeons primarily because there were few reliable anaesthetics available at that time. However just as hypnosis was catching on as a general anaesthetic more powerful and reliable drugs were discovered and medical hypnosis was left behind.

The diary of Dr. James Esdale, a British doctor practicing in India, describes over 1000 operations during the years 1845 - 1851 using hypnosis as the only anaesthetic. Of his three hundred major operations nineteen were amputations, none of his patients experienced post-operative trauma. His letter to the British Medical Board reporting his successes was never acknowledged.

The French neurologist, Jean Charcot, used hypnosis in the treatment of hysteria. His lectures became so popular that even the famous psychiatrist, Sigmund Freud, attended. Freud himself used hypnosis in his clinical work. Not having the patience to go through the long induction process (inducing a hypnotic trance in the patient) he would direct an attendant to perform the inductions. Once they were in a light trance he would enter to conduct his therapy. Freud later abandoned hypnosis for his 'free association' method of psychoanalysis.

Today medical hypnosis, now named 'Clinical Hypnotherapy', remains quite misunderstood by the medical profession and lay people alike. The misinterpretation of this incredible tool by the popular media and entertainment industry will continue to keep hypnosis in the grey area of fringe medicine and quackery.

Trance States

The hypnotic trance is described as 'body asleep - mind aware'. The trance state feels as though you are half asleep just before waking or just as you drift off to sleep. It may feel like you are physically floating and you have almost no awareness of your physical body. Your mind slows and you may begin to day-dream. Just the sound of the therapist's voice keeps you from drifting off to sleep. Catching this powerful state is the task of the hypnotherapist and yours as you learn self hypnosis.

Your body is, to all intents and purposes asleep but the mind remains aware. You will remember what is said, hear external sounds and are quite capable of exercising free will.

The trance state is categorised into light, medium and deep. Most clinical hypnotherapy is done in the light trance state simply because people want their problem to be cured in as short a time as possible. They often believe that it only takes a single session. For most problems of a non-neurotic or psychotic type this is possible. A light trance state is also invaluable when asking the client questions that require a verbal reply. If the trance is deepened then the verbal capacity is reduced until only a whisper is heard – if that.

A deep trance is useful in experiencing a floating, dream-like sensation and is used to implant post hypnotic suggestions. Unfortunately the client is unable to reply in such a deep state and will soon fall asleep. I use this state when a client is exhausted and a good deep sleep will help reduce their stress and fatigue.

Not everyone will reach this state. It may take many months of hard dedicated practice. However, you have experienced trance many times in your life. Watching TV is likened to entering the body asleep (no physical awareness) and mind aware state. When you read a good book you become so absorbed in the story that you can enter it – this is a trance-like experience. Performing a repetitive task or concentrating on an activity requiring detailed work, like drawing or washing the dishes, may create a similar effect. This creative state is akin to the light trance state.

You have been in a light trance state so many times that you might want to use this as a trigger, a means to recall the sensation of relaxation. This can then open the door for you to go into a deeper state.

Why use hypnosis as therapy?

Studies have shown that the hypnotic trance state is not necessary for improving performance. They have also shown that it does, however, enhance learning and reduces tension. This is not really a contradiction as it shows that some people can achieve remarkable feats with or without the aid of self hypnosis or hypnotherapy. It is, however, an extremely useful tool in psychotherapy to teach clients how to relax and how to use this state for healing as well as in resolving psychological issues. This book will show you in some detail how to do this.

Suggestion and the placebo effect

In 1981 Dr Lenard (USA) gave his dying cancer patient a trial drug which subsequently cured him of his disease, lymphosarcoma. However, when the patient heard that the drug was no longer thought to be effective in lymphosarcoma he began to show symptoms and progressively became ill again. At his next visit Dr Lenard convinced him that this was not true and the patient again made a rapid recovery after being given injections of sterile water. The patient continued his recovery until he heard again that the drug was useless. He died 2 days later. Suggestion is powerful.

Placebo studies demonstrate that we all respond to varying degrees of suggestion:

- The worse it tastes the better it is.

- Small pills are more potent than large ones.
- Injections are more powerful than pills or liquids.
- Placebo crosses all socio-economic and intellectual boundaries.

Conscious vs Unconscious - the power of belief

Trance states are often referred to as 'unconscious states' suggesting that we have both a conscious and an unconscious mind. Confused? Even the science of psychology cannot agree upon a single definition for 'consciousness'. To assist in understanding the hypnotic state it helps to accept or agree to accept that we have two worlds: a conscious one that we exist in when awake and an unconscious one that we enter when asleep or day dreaming. I tell my clients that we live in two worlds: one when our eyes are open and the other when we close them. Our eyes are the simple switch to changing states.

The conscious state is the interface we use when awake. In this state we critically analyse our daily experiences. In the trance state, which is the unconscious state, suggestions are no longer effectively screened so suggestion and guided imagery are able to gain traction.

Belief is a powerful force that you can fine-tune to improve your performance in any field you chose. A positive belief leads to positive states and positive performances. These act to reinforce the initial positive belief.

Who should I see for clinical hypnotherapy?

There are highly respected organisations that endeavour to maintain the practice of hypnosis at a professional level. Each country has an organisation with strict guidelines and criteria of entry. Many psychologists and medical practitioners use clinical hypnotherapy.

Always ask to see their qualifications before you accept someone as your therapist. Hypnotherapists believe that you do not need to be a medical practitioner to practice hypnotherapy. In fact many people prefer a non-medical hypnotherapist.

Hypnosis and meditation: Are they both the same state?

After many years of personal and professional experience working with clients and students, I have concluded there is essentially no difference between the hypnotic state and meditation. Both feel the same and both can be induced through the same techniques.

Traditionally meditation aims to guide the client into altered states of consciousness for spiritual, psychological or health reasons. Clinical hypnotherapy on the other hand is usually used for improving performance in specific areas of sports, pain control, stress management and study.

In my practice I modified my approach to clinical hypnotherapy to become what I now call 'inner work'. Inner work is simply a guided meditation using a light trance. It aims to take a client into their imaginal or inner world to achieve specific therapeutic goals. The stories you read in this book are all forms of what I call 'inner work'.

The value of deep state relaxation and 'inner work' is such that I encourage my clients to practice their self hypnosis techniques every day - sometimes I recommend they practice the CD I hand them four or more times a day. I always have a chuckle when they tell me that I put them to sleep at night.

Techniques used by traditional clinical hypnotherapists may be different from more liberal therapists. My background in psychodynamic psychotherapy, tai chi and Taoist meditation has helped me develop a variety of alternative relaxation techniques. I also use my knowledge of astrology and tarot to introduce those who are interested to meet and work with their archetypes.

TAME YOUR MIND

"The road to success is always under construction." Anthony Robbins.

Self hypnosis is the practice of entering a trance state without the guidance of another. In fact all hypnosis is self hypnosis because you permit yourself to enter trance. If you practice these exercises diligently you can develop the ability to go within and to create specific programs when you need greater control in difficult life situations.

All the exercises in this book demonstrate what can be done in this trance state. The more you practice the basics of relaxation the greater your chance of success. Self hypnosis can be a life-time skill but you need dedication, commitment and to practice daily.

Remember: commitment + deliberate practice = success.

The woman who lived inside a pyramid

Before I start this section I would like to tell you of a client of mine who suffered from Meniere's Disease. It was so severe it prevented her leaving her house for the twelve months before I saw her. She told me that she usually spent all day in bed. Going anywhere, even to the bathroom, caused her to become dizzy, fall to the floor and vomit. Her life was an endless torture.

At our first session I did a basic hypnotherapy induction just to demonstrate that she could relax. Then, at the next session, I came up with the idea that she could live safely inside a stable, grounded pyramid. I explained that if she imagined herself inside a pyramid then it's incredible stability may help her stand without becoming dizzy.

During our next session she proudly described how she was now walking fine. But there was a problem: the pyramid was opaque and she couldn't see out of it. That was simple, we transformed it into a transparent pyramid that she could easily see out of.

This may have been the pivotal point because when I saw her next she smiled and told me that she had walked to the shopping centre - across a busy six lane highway. I was horrified and tried to explain that she was only beginning to recover and that she needed to go slowly and not charge into things like that. To no avail I might add because there was no stopping this dynamic 65 year old grandmother.

At each subsequent session she would tell me of a problem she had. I would guide her into trance and she would role play until it resolved itself. Such things as: vacuuming - each time she bent forwards she felt nauseous and dizzy - fixed; she loved doing jigsaw puzzles but they gave her the same symptoms - fixed; washing up - fixed. Together we resolved each new issue in a single session. This woman was one of the most incredible women I have ever met and until I lost contact with her some fifteen years later she was still walking inside her pyramid.

Goal setting - Preparation for self hypnosis

Goal setting has been proven to save time, increase performance and improve your ability to achieve success. Before starting self hypnosis take the time to write down exactly what you want from it.

To talk the language of the unconscious you need to learn to 'speak' it's sensory language. The three most important senses are sight (visual images), sounds (as well as vocalisations, what is said and what you are saying to yourself in your head) and feelings. Combining all three makes this a most powerful tool and is the best way to program and create your goals.

Here is a step by step way to create goals using this process:

(1) Write out a list of the things you want to achieve.

(2) Prioritise them.

(3) Take the first one and create an image and include it's associated sounds and feelings of yourself achieving that goal.

To be more specific this includes:

3rd person perspective

- observe yourself achieving the goal from a perspective outside yourself

- create images of the setting as well as a close up of yourself

- make the image clear, full colour and bright

- associate sounds with the setting and your goal

- add comments that you expect to hear from others, for example, words of encouragement or praise

- make the suggestions powerful by adding emotional emphasis with some passion, make it exciting and enjoyable

1st person perspective

- visualise as though you are now in the image achieving your goal

- look from your own eyes and make the images full colour and as real as possible

- say the words you would normally say to yourself as you achieve your goal

- make the words sound strong and full of pride, excitement and vitality

- feel yourself within the setting: the sunshine, a slight breeze, feet on the ground, even smell the fragrances of the flowers. The goal is to be in the moment, work hard at this

- feel the emotions of pride and success as they surge through your body, up your spine and into your chest

- feel yourself a winner

(4) Journal your experiences so you can reflect on it later.

(5) Create a cartoon style portrayal of each sense's role in achieving each goal.

(6) Be flexible and prepared to change and adapt the goal or the format as you improve.

(7) Practice your self hypnosis program described above twice each day.

(8) Use this process when making up your own self hypnosis audios.

TECHNIQUES, SCRIPTS AND AUDIO'S

Inducing the trance state can be done in any number of ways. I will script the most common techniques that can assist you. But first, remember to do your goal setting as listed above.

Suggestions, programs and affirmations

Most psychotherapists consider every act to be the result of our unconscious programs, urges, instincts and drives. If they remain unresolved they can become our untamed dragons. These programs can be as basic as fight, flight or freeze, or as complex as those used in our relationships.

We all pick up our programs like sticky fly paper: haphazardly and without any conscious planning or consideration. Through processes like self hypnosis you can re-program using imagery and suggestion. You can grow into the person you want to become by understanding how your mind operates and then creating and running more enlightened programs.

Right brain language - talking the language of the unconscious

As I mentioned previously our mind operates on the five senses. The strongest senses are visual, auditory (words and sounds) and kinesthetic (physical sensations and emotional feelings). By using these senses in your self hypnosis you maximise your transfer of desire to the unconscious mind. Although all senses are important it is best to discover which sense is your strongest. From there you can springboard from your strongest sense to experience the others.

If you are strongly visual you can use that modality by first creating an image and then introducing the other senses as you engage and achieve your goal. Auditory is usually strongest for those that like to listen to poetry or music to relax. They love to use the sounds of waves or the wind in the trees to fall asleep. The kinesthetic (sense of touch) enjoy feeling the rocking motion of a hammock or feeling the sun on their face. This is sometimes the hardest to develop but is very powerful. The kinesthetic body is what we can develop for healing, dream work, astral travel and out-of-body experiences.

Use your strongest sense to go into trance then you will find that the other senses become easier. It's when in the deepest states that all senses come alive especially the kinesthetic or dream body.

Self Hypnosis Progressive Relaxation Script

WARNING: DO NOT LISTEN TO THIS SECTION WHILE DRIVING OR OPERATING MACHINERY.

Find yourself in a comfortable position in a quiet place free from distractions and noises. Turn off your mobile phone and put a sign on your door. Close your eyes and give your mind, body and spirit permission to relax. Now allow yourself to let go and flow with the experience.

Take three slow, deep breaths. As you release each breath imagine and feel yourself sinking into the bed / chair deeper and deeper as you let go of any stress and tension. Feel it. With each exhalation feel heavier and heavier releasing tension with every breath.

Relax your eyes - they feel so tired, all they want to do is roll back into your head as you go deeper and deeper into a deep sleep. Next your eyebrows, forehead, temples, cheeks, lips and jaw. Slowly dwell on each part until it starts to feel relaxed and heavy. Then relaxing your whole head, neck and throat. As you relax you start to feel that lovely sleepy feeling as you enter into a deeper relaxed state.

Relax your shoulders, upper arms, elbows, wrists and hands. Now both arms and hands feel heavy and relaxed - again go slowly. Relax down your body until you get to the soles of your feet, both feet and legs feel heavy and relaxed.

Switching off - now go through the same process from head to feet, switching the body parts off just as quickly as you would a light switch. This is a more advanced technique and may take a lot of practice before you can do this quickly. Don't fret if it takes time.

Your body feels as though it is light and floating. Combine your breath with each switch. As you breathe out switch off that body part so you develop an association between exhalation and the switching off command.

Now count back from five to zero and switch off even deeper. 5 is the head; 4 is neck, throat, shoulders and arms; 3 is chest, shoulder blades and upper back; 2 is stomach, pelvis and lower back; 1 is legs and feet; 0 is the soles of the feet. You may do this set several times to go deeper. This is known as the deepening stage in trance induction. With time and practice you will be able to switch off instantly.

Trigger words - by this time you are in a deeply relaxed state. Softly say to yourself the trigger words: **"relax now, relax now, relax now"**. As you do so, feel yourself switch off immediately into a deep trance state - deeply asleep. Combine your exhalations with the "relax now" command and it can become even more powerful. Each time you use these trigger words you will enter into trance easier and quicker. You can use this trigger to relax in stressful situations but you will not fall asleep. This takes practice. Ensure that you imagine that you are switching off quickly at the beginning. As you get better it will no longer be imagination but reality.

Imagery - as you relax into a deep trance state or deep sleep find yourself on a beach, in a garden or some special sanctuary. This will act as a place for your healing and to further practice your trance skills. Next use your five senses to their fullest. See clearly, hear clearly, feel, smell and taste. Make an effort to get into and stay in this sanctuary. This sanctuary can be a place where you learn more about yourself and do the magical things you have planned.

Goal setting - now imagine a hammock or a perfect place to lie down and allow yourself to enter an even deeper trance. Use the switching off technique as you let go. Create your goals using imagery and suggestions and the 3rd and 1st person perspectives.

I encourage my clients to fall asleep for a few minutes at the end, it helps to consolidate the session.

Come back to consciousness slowly, or count from 1 to 3. On 3 you wake up feeling fresh and relaxed. Give yourself the command to remember everything that happened while under self hypnosis.

This script can be modified to suit your personality, ability, interests and needs.

Creating the future - for specific day to day situations

For specific goals first complete the goal setting exercise so you know exactly what you want to create or achieve.

Enter the trance state using whatever method works for you. Imagine yourself being that person of the future doing the things that you want to do. Use the 3rd and 1st person perspective described previously.

For instance: I once worked with a particularly horrific boss. I could barely stand the thought of working with her. She continually triggered some of my own inner dragons, I could imagine them fighting among themselves whenever conflict arose in our working relationship. I am not an assertive person so I decided to change things using the techniques described in this book.

I visualised her happy and relaxed in situations that would normally trigger conflict. After this exercise we got along quite well and our difficulties all but disappeared. I used this technique every day for months, eventually it worked and we got along fine.

Creating the future - self-esteem and assertiveness

Use your favourite technique to enter trance. Imagine an image of yourself (3rd person perspective) looking and being exactly the way you would like to look and be. You can see yourself in full colour, bright lighting, a close up of your face smiling and confident wearing the clothes you want to wear. Watch yourself for a while in situations where you would like to be more confident and in control. Observe yourself as you act exactly the way you want to act in those situations. Keep practicing until recreating your imagery is easy.

Next enter your future self (1st person) and 'feel' the power, confidence, self control and determination you now possess. You can add any specific personality characteristics you want as you experience or imagine your own future. Spend some time experiencing how this new You acts in situations that would normally be stressful for you. Act powerful and assertive but without losing the compassion and loving personality you already possess.

Musicians for instance, in the lead up to a performance, they will often visualise arriving at the venue, sitting backstage, tuning the instrument, walking onto the stage and performing the piece. The mental rehearsal can boost their confidence and ability to perform well on stage.

The Yellow Brick Road

This is a gentle, non-specific goal setting exercise. Imagine a brilliant golden path stretching ahead of you just like the one Dorothy walks along with her friends in the movie, The Wizard of Oz. Add rainbows, flowers and anything else you wish to place on your path. This path represents your journey through life and it just gets better and brighter as you travel along it.

If you glance behind you will see the barriers, the side turns you took and the stumbling blocks. The important thing to note is that these are all behind you. Ahead, things are beautiful and life is just getting better. Sometimes if you travel forward in time you will catch a glimpse of the wonderful adventures awaiting in your future.

By using this technique regularly you impress upon your unconscious what you really want out of life: *"Now pay attention unconscious. This is what I want you to work on and create for me. A pleasurable life that is just getting better and better each day."*

Eye catalepsy

This technique is simple and easy to learn. Fix your gaze on any object that is slightly above eye level. You can choose a spot on the ceiling, the wall or focus on a painting.

By making your eyes tired you can eventually become fatigued and start to close them automatically. Now try it with the internal command to 'relax now' until your eyes close automatically. Practice this tired eyes relaxation every day for a week or two and you will find yourself entering the self hypnotic state easier. I sometimes use a highlighter pen and draw it towards my face. As it gets closer to my eyes, my eyes start to close. When it touches my forehead I let go completely and fall into a light trance.

Inner space landscapes - lake, moon and candle

I use this myself just for a change to my usual techniques. Imagine sitting by the edge of a large lake just on dusk. There is a slight breeze ruffling the lake's surface. Rising directly opposite you is a full moon. As you relax with each breath you notice the moon rising slowly with its silvery trail appearing on the water. The deeper you go into trance the calmer the lake surface becomes. You soon notice that the moon becomes brighter and its reflection on the water's surface is like a stairway to the stars.

Here is an alternative:

Imagine yourself sitting in a cave and in front of you is a clear pool of water. The cave is dark and stalactites and stalagmites cover the floor and ceilings. It is an old cave that generations of monks have used for meditation training over the centuries. On the opposite side of the pool is a single candle. Calmly gaze at the candle's reflection in the pool of water in front of you. Every ten seconds or so a drop of water falls from a stalactite above into the pool creating a ripple. As you enter a deeper state of trance the ripple lasts for shorter and shorter periods. Eventually you will drift off into some very peaceful states.

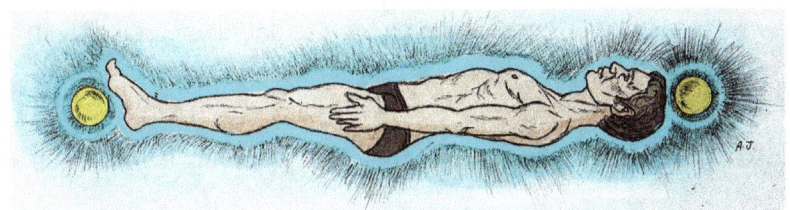

The Alpha Omega Cocoon

This is for deep meditative states and a favourite of mine for healing and balancing negative emotions during stressful periods. It also acts to prevent negative thoughts.

When you enter the self hypnotic state imagine a ball of light just below the soles of your feet. Focus on how warm it feels on your feet and ankles. Imagine any stress and tension flowing out of your body through the soles of your feet into this ball of light. If you can, breathe out into the ball of light from the soles of your feet.

Above your head is another bright ball of light radiating warmth over your head and shoulders. It's important to involve all your senses especially the feeling or kinesthetic sense. Feel warm, bright energy flowing gently into your body from these two balls of light.

Now imagine filaments of silken light spinning and weaving from one ball to the other creating a cocoon of light around your body. This is just like a silk worm's cocoon complete with golden threads of silk. The diameter of the cocoon can be about your arms length away from you - larger or smaller depending on what you prefer.

Now relax inside your protective cocoon and feel yourself glowing brightly like a radiant light globe.

Those practitioners who can feel the energy flowing from their body into the balls of light (above the head and below the feet) generally find it easier to enter a deep trance state. Some people float out of their body at this stage.

Just remember your key is to let go physically, mentally, emotionally and spiritually.

Fantasy Island

One lonely pensioner, Vera, accidentally closed the door on her pet bird, Geordie. She had also lost her daughter to suicide a few years before. Vera was depressed and quite in need of emotional healing. We used trance to create an island sanctuary. On that island appeared her little budgie and all of her other pets that had passed on over the years.

Vera visited her island in self hypnosis every day where she was able to resolve her guilt for killing her pet budgie. She then went on to heal the hurts and unresolved issues with her daughter. Vera was able to structure her healing by seeing her daughter at an age when things were going nicely for her before the abductions and abuse.

She gave her daughter a happy childhood on the island. Together they were able to establish a relationship that helped heal them both. Vera practiced every day and eventually was able to develop and use the island extensively on her own.

As she became more confident she invited her deceased son and then her mother and father to her fantasy island. There was unfinished business with them too.

At first she spent most of her spare time on the islands but slowly as her life became more comfortable she only visited when needed. When she does visit it is just a quick, *"Hello, Geordie."* before rushing off to visit her family on other islands that she'd created.

Some years later in one of my own meditations I visited Vera's island. On the top of the hill in the darkness of night I could just make out some small furry animals as well as her birds, cats and dogs. I asked Vera at our next session if she also had rabbits as pets.

"Yes, I always had rabbits when I was young," she said, *"I'd forgotten all about them."*

Making your own scripts and audio clips

This is probably the best way to speed up your trance induction process. You can use your computer or mobile phone to record yourself, or someone else, reading your script aloud. Add some background music if you wish. These audios can help you stay on task and not wander off too much. It is also a great way to place specific and directed new programs into your unconscious.

- Prepare your goals using the goal setting exercise

- Write out your script to last 10 - 20 minutes

- Include specific sensory suggestions

- Practice reading into your recorder - try to get it to flow

- Find a source of music or environmental sounds to provide a peaceful background. This could be classical music, specific relaxation music, natural sounds or whatever works to help you relax. Research shows that vocals can distract relaxation and interfere with short term memory. If you are using your script for study and self hypnosis it is recommended you use non-vocal music

- Put on the background music and start talking in a relaxed slow voice. With practice you will find the right 'voice' to use. If your recorder allows you can mix them separately using free software like Audacity or Garage Band

- Make a separate recording for each program or goal

- Don't try to learn too many programs at once. Our unconscious takes time to change, but do make as many audios as you want

- Practice daily for at least 2 weeks, you can change the program at any time if it needs it

INNER SPACE - HEALING

'Give a person a fish and you feed them for a day; teach them how to fish and you feed them for life.'

Keeping yourself healthy is undeniably a worthwhile lifetime ambition. If you accept responsibility for your health then you may become a little more vigilant in what you eat, think and do. Perhaps make it a habit to listen to what people with knowledge of health have to say: observe and put into practice what works for you.

"A journey of a thousand miles begins with the first step" is an old Chinese saying. It may remind you that the moment you take responsibility for your health you have taken that first step.

Please don't think that you will be healed immediately, my aim in writing this section is to introduce you to techniques that may be used in conjunction with your usual medical treatment.

Medical studies and imagery

Studies have shown that personality types may specifically contribute to illness and recovery. For example:

- Type A personalities (high pressure living) may have more heart attacks.

- The martyr personality may develop illness faster.

- Low self-esteem and self image may negate attempts to heal.

- Unresolved grief may lead to reduced immune responses and disease.

- Depression and feelings of helplessness and hopelessness may precipitate illness.

Technique For Healing Using Self Hypnosis

- Write out your health goals and the images you will be using in your self hypnosis program (visuals, sounds and feelings).

- Practice entering the trance state, body and mind relaxed and aware, several times each day.

- Practice your self hypnosis healing program using your goals and imagery from point one above.

- Create your image as described below:

3rd person perspective:- Visualise an image of yourself in a state of perfect health. Make the image a close up, bright, full sunlight, clear, strong colours. Hear the sounds associated with where you are in the image: birds in the trees, people enthusiastically congratulating you on your health, etc.

1st person perspective:- Now enter that image: look through your own eyes, see everything as clear as possible. Hear the words or phrases (suggestions or affirmations) you would say to yourself as you attain this state of health. Make the words happy and enthusiastic. You can use them as a trigger for increasing health and vitality at other times too. Feel yourself achieving your goal. Feel the emotions of pride, joy, love of life and the surge of vitality.

- Relax again after this exercise and allow yourself to float back to awareness. Reinforce your goal by feeling better, happier and reinforce your desire to practice this exercise on a daily basis.

- See yourself rising from this session healthier and happier than when you started.

- Practice twice each day for at least the first two weeks. You can then modify your self hypnosis program according to your needs.

Feeling vitality in health

The kinesthetic or feeling sense is of vital importance in healing. Visualising an image of yourself healed is powerful but the reality of it can be a very long time in coming. Using the first person perspective and feeling your life force flowing and surging through you is the pinnacle of self healing. If you can emphasise this in your self hypnosis you are on the road to recovery.

Life force (chi) - what does it feel like?

Tai chi, the Chinese moving meditation, and yoga emphasise the flow of life force (chi or prana) through the body. The Chinese say that we have a number of lines or meridians that carry energy through our body energising and harmonising the internal organs. This flow of energy is absolutely essential to the maintenance of health and longevity. The cultivation of energy could become a lifetime exercise and an enjoyable one at that. With practice it is possible for you to 'breathe' or flow this energy through your body. It feels like a shiver or a warm current of air or an electric tingling, thickening sensation. It is different for each individual. The best explanation I can give is that it feels like a shiver and is excruciatingly pleasurable.

The healing hand

Enter a light trance state and imagine that your body is hollow. Your life force is flowing from your heart or chest cavity, down your arm and into your hand. Allow your hand to feel warm, thick and tingling. Take a few slow deep breaths and imagine that your hand is as light as a feather as it floats towards any area of pain or disease that needs healing. Imagine warm healing energy flowing through your hand and into your body healing and rejuvenating each and every cell. Emphasise the kinesthetic / feeling faculty as well as visualising the healing energy flowing into each cell. Practice daily and when you go to bed at night.

Space invaders

Imagine yourself with mini-warriors armed with powerful lasers wiping out your invading germs, viruses or diseased cells. Make it as real as possible and use both the 3rd and 1st person perspective. One client I worked with would fly his fire-breathing dragon through his body so that the dragon's flames would destroy his diseased cells. Another has hundreds of happy little creatures that run around his body placing their hands on his injured cells to heal them.

Body Scanning

This is an examination of your physical body while in the trance state. Using your favourite technique enter a light trance and imagine your physical body. Now scan it with your mind for any injuries. If you have trouble visualising send your mind on a journey around the body 'feeling' every organ, muscle and bone for injury.

This is an especially useful technique for sports people prone to injuries. I have a friend that uses this method to scan his race horses for injuries after training and racing. He is very accurate and it saves time and money on vet fees. It has helped him become one of Australia's most successful horse trainers. With practice you can become quite good at this technique.

Tension and migraine headaches

Headaches are one of the most common of all human complaints and some forms may be eased through the use of self hypnosis. Studies show that sustained muscular tension in the shoulders, neck and face are some of the main contributors to chronic tension headaches.

The cause of migraines is still debated in the scientific literature. Current research indicates that hormone levels in the blood may be the cause for many sufferers. Whatever the cause the practice of deep relaxation (deep trance) can have the effect of reducing the severity and time you suffer with your migraines.

Solutions for tension headaches are well within the realm of self hypnosis especially if you can go into a moderate to deep trance before it fully takes hold. With daily practice you may be able to prevent headaches before they fully develop.

One client had severe migraines of which I wasn't even aware. She wanted assistance for stress so we began the first session with a deep relaxation. She called back three days later to say that she no longer had the migraine at the back of her eye which had been bothering her for the past two years. Please note that migraines and headaches certainly do not always respond to self hypnosis so make sure you see your medical professional as well.

Glove anaesthesia

Enter a light trance and imagine one of your hands has a glove placed over it. Now imagine it becoming completely anaesthetised with no feeling at all. Slowly move your hand to where the pain is and let it touch. Imagine the anaesthetising sensation flowing from your hand into the painful area. This is an old technique not commonly used these days as pain is now recognised as a warning that something is wrong and needs attention. Please use it with that in mind.

Childbirth

Childbirth is not an illness but a lot of women worry so much it makes them ill. Proper care from a health professional is essential. The challenge is to have a relaxed and healthy pregnancy and a pain free delivery. Use your goal setting to first determine what you want from your self hypnosis. Next I suggest you take the following steps:

• Enter a deeply relaxed state on a daily basis. This is good for both you and your baby and helps manage blood pressure and stress levels. Perhaps your partner could guide you.

• First visualise walking out of the hospital with your baby in your arms, happy, smiling and obviously feeling terrific. Your unconscious interprets this as the whole birthing process went very well, was smooth and pain free.

- During pregnancy use imagery to see your child healthy and happy. Send her or him love by imagining your heart centre warm and then flow that warmth into your womb and baby.

- Practice going into a deep trance two to three times a day prior to the two weeks before delivery. You can add imagery of your smiling baby in your arms straight after delivery as well. Your unconscious will interpret this as a safe delivery because you are both smiling, comfortable and pain free.

- Pain control may be achieved by using 'glove anaesthesia' described above. This is a process of imagining that wherever you place your hand, will be completely anaesthetised. Or imagine that the painful area is flowing with healing light and warmth. Don't try to be the martyr though and refuse drugs if you really need them. Use common sense and listen to the advice of your midwife in this matter.

Throughout pregnancy and the birthing process always report any concerns or issues to your medical professional. This is not a substitute for their advice but an adjunct to their care.

Pain control

In some cases we are in a situation in which we are unable to get relief from pain. Cases of bone injury, severe accidents, toothache, bruising, burns and the like will respond with varying degrees of success to self hypnosis. If you have been practicing self hypnosis for some time it will be much easier to use for pain management. If you are already in pain and try self hypnosis you may find that it doesn't work very well.

I was asked to aid a brave young lady, Libby, dying of liver and bone cancer. Her doctor had no more to offer and the hospital staff had resorted to morphine to ease her pain towards the end.

Libby and her husband refused to give up hope and began a course of Chinese herbs that had helped other sufferers. They tried to reduce the daily morphine to allow the herbs to work faster. But the pain continually broke through as her cancer had progressed to a critical point.

When I arrived I was distressed to see Libby in continual pain and unable to sit or lie in the one position for longer than a few seconds. I started by inducing a trance state with eye catalepsy (making the eyes tired through staring at an object) and she went into a light trance easily. But within a few minutes she was back due to the intense pain of the advanced cancer.

I visited Libby every day for four days before I had to return home. During this time Libby was entering some very blissful and spiritual spaces during self hypnosis. She was also experiencing surges of energy through her body. We were quietly hopeful of a slow recovery.

The following week I was back and she told me that she just had three days without pain. We were ecstatic but this was short-lived.

While Libby did not recover she was able to experience moments of relief from pain.

Out-of-body - for pain management

Enter trance and imagine yourself above your body and looking down upon it. Feel its nice floating sensations. While out of your body you are able to remain detached from the pain. This is experienced by many people involved in disasters and accidents witnessing events as if they were above and to the side of their physical body. Some have spiritual experiences that confirms their religious beliefs or initiates a deeper love and acceptance of their place in the universe. Libby was able to experience some special moments while in this state.

Post operative recovery

Hypnosis has often been cited as beneficial in aiding patients recovering from illness or surgery. The essential aspect is to allow yourself ample time to prepare yourself mentally before the operation through regular self hypnosis exercises. Consider the type of result you want then create it using your goal setting process.

Post operative healing with self hypnosis is no different to many of the other processes outlined in this book. Set your goal and then prepare for it to actualise into reality. In many cases you may be able to activate your healing energy potential. By activating this healing force your recovery time may be significantly reduced.

Chi breathing, the thymus gland and boosting your immune system

The thymus gland is known as the "Heart Centre" or "Heart Chakra" in yoga and other eastern spiritual systems. It is now accepted as being one of the glands responsible for generating and maintaining a healthy immune response. Up until the mid 1970's the function of the thymus gland was relatively unknown. Now we understand that it produces hormones that stimulate the production of antibodies in the spleen and lymph systems, phagocytes which devour viruses and microbes and T cells which destroy unhealthy tissues like cancerous tumours.

Studies have shown a link between happiness and health. As the Heart Centre is the seat of love, joy and happiness we now know why.

The Thymus Tap

Step 1 - getting started

Locate the thymus or Heart Centre in the middle of your sternum about four finger breadths down from the collar bone (the two prominent bones below your voice box). Very gently tap rhythmically with your finger tips for some seconds or until it feels slightly warm. You can also use the "Healing Hand" technique describer earlier and place it on your Heart Centre and allow warmth to penetrate into your thymus. This is the initial stimulation or "awakening" of your immune system's heart centre.

Step 2 - breathing

Enter your relaxed self hypnotic state and concentrate on your breath - a normal relaxed breath. Now imagine that you are breathing through the Heart Centre / thymus gland in and out. Imagine it as warm and stimulating and after a while you may begin to actually feel the flow of energy radiating outwards filling your chest cavity. This is a warm and often joyful, loving experience.

Step 3 - visualisation

Visualise your heart centre / thymus gland glowing brightly. You can use white or golden light or any colour that comes to you. Allow this to penetrate through your chest cavity and to radiate outwards surrounding you as a glowing aura.

Step 4 - combining them

Now combine all three steps in the one session. The tapping, warmth, visualisation and the energy breathing. When this happens you may actually feel a shiver or radiant warmth filling your chest cavity. Allow this to keep radiating until you can guide it into the part of your body that needs healing energy. I like to imagine every cell receiving this life force waking up, stretching, beaming with joy as they soak up this glorious healing light.

Step 5 - chi breathing on location

You can try breathing this energy directly through that part of your body that is diseased or injured basically anywhere. Use the same method of breathing and visualisation as above. You might find that you don't even need to do the thymus tapping first. You can even use this method for sports injuries.

Practice this technique every day. Don't think that it will happen immediately though. It took me years to work out this technique for myself. Make it a daily health ritual and you will have your inner physician on call 24 hours a day.

As a demonstration of the healing effect of energy I was with a friend when a visitor walked into the house her fingers bruised and crushed. When this woman arrived she accidentally closed the car door on her fingers. Her keys were still in the ignition and the car doors were locked. After nearly ten minutes of calling for help the neighbours across the street heard her cries.

The moment she walked in we saw her discoloured and swollen fingers. They looked badly damaged, like blue sausages. My friends were both hands-on healers and they rushed her into their healing room. There they held their "healing hands" on hers. After half an hour she emerged with all bruising and swelling gone. I was truly amazed.

Although hypnosis and the trance state is very powerful you may also consider factors that may contribute to your illness. Radiation from power lines, electric blankets, microwaves; toxic chemical exposure from insecticides, fungicides, pesticides, food colours, preservatives; heavy metals like aluminium, lead, mercury, cadmium. Lack of exercise and a poor diet contribute too. If you continue to expose yourself to these powerful health reducing elements then all the trance healing in the world will help but not cure your problem.

Healing - sometimes it's more difficult than you expect

I would like to share a story of a special person with whom I worked. She entered my office as an aged fifty five year old lady. I soon found out that she had lost her mother when she was fifteen years old and she had never really recovered. A year prior to seeing me she had developed a mild heart problem which triggered depression. With the depression she was affected with constant migraines, sadness and was soon crying most of every day. Her family were worried.

In her current state she was heading for a stroke or heart attack. I thought to myself, "*I need to do something for this poor woman.*" I decided that I might be able to lift some of her grief by taking her into her inner world to meet her inner self.

I guided her to close her eyes and to go and find herself from twelve moths ago. She then gave herself a hug and brought her back into her life. She did this very easily and was able to recall her younger happier self. They hugged and she cried some more tears.

When she came back to consciousness she was very happy and she smiled for the first time. We then talked about losing her mother and she said that she really wanted to visit her mother now. So why not? It worked once why shouldn't this work twice?

I said. "*Close your eyes and find your mother, you can visit her in heaven. Can you feel her hugging you? Can you see her beautiful smile?*"

She nodded between her tears of joy. That's what often happens when doing this therapy and I am quite used to that. But when she came back she didn't stop sobbing.

I thought to myself, "*Oh dear, have I made you even more unsettled by taking you into your inner world? I've opened Pandora's Box of loss and grief. What will I tell her family if she doesn't stop crying?*"

I patted her back and talked to her and eventually gave her a hug. She stopped crying and looked up at me. Through her tears she said that she now realised how she had been living in fear of reaching fifty six years of age. That was when her mother died.

"*I didn't know,*" she kept repeating because she didn't know that this was why she was felling so depressed these past twelve months.

She hadn't realised that her migraines and depression had everything to do with her own mortality and the loss of her mother at the age she was about to reach. Each day she was closer to the same age as her mother when she passed away.

I gave her a drink of water and then she took out her mobile phone to call her husband. Then she ran out and brought in her family who were in the waiting room. She was so excited, so alive, smiling and happy. This is what is called a 'catharsis' or 'abreaction', a release of psychic tension. When it happens it's dramatic and incredibly effective. Her homework was to practice her self hypnosis CD daily.

That was one of the most fulfilling experiences of my career but I was too exhausted to enjoy it at that exact moment - I just felt enormous relief. I saw her a month later after she had come back from an overseas holiday with her family and she was radiant. Sometimes, I remind myself, it pays to follow my instincts.

CHILDREN

Children are our future. We invest all our love into their upbringing and feel their every scratch and bruise. Teaching your child to relax is something that would benefit both your child and yourself. As easy as it may sound teaching children self hypnosis or meditation may sometimes prove to be a difficult task. After all wouldn't you rather be out playing than sitting or lying down listening to someone telling you to relax?

My approach, and I have three children of my own (and now two grandchildren), was to offer to help but I did not push the issue. Self development is best made available as and when your child is ready. Story telling and guided imagery is what I prefer to a basic relaxation approach. Following are some situations when direct assistance is very helpful.

Nightmares and night terrors

There are two kinds of night-time frights: *nightmares* in which your child is having a scary dream and is easily wakened. *Night terrors* are when your child doesn't wake up and is still asleep. They might walk and mumble and are stuck in an inner world. It can be frightening to watch.

Night terrors are best treated by sitting quietly and talking to your child calmly until they settle. They rarely wake but often go back to sleep after about ten minutes. When they wake in the morning they rarely remember anything.

Overheating is frequently the cause of night terrors. Observe and see if this fixes your child's problem as it did for my children. Just wait until they fall asleep then pull back some of their blankets for a while to allow them to cool off. After ten to twenty minutes they have gone past the point of overheating and you can replace some of their blankets. This is what I did for our children and it stopped those frightening night terrors immediately.

When the body and head overheat it causes visual and auditory hallucinations just like a person suffering from sunstroke. In the case of sunstroke the treatment is to immediately cool the sufferer down until they regain consciousness. In the case of a child suffering night terrors check to see if they are sweating and hot to the touch. If so, cool them down with a fan or cover their forehead with a cool wet cloth.

Overheating can be dangerous particularly in summer when a child wraps themselves in layers of blankets. Remove some of their blankets over the course of a few days until you find the right number to stop the night terrors and still keep them warm. Electric blankets are another possibility, make sure it is turned off when they go to bed – or remove it completely.

Imagery for nightmares

Nightmares are not night terrors - remember that they are quite different and require different approaches. This exercise is often best conducted during the day. Children love to pretend and are often better at visual imagery and imagination than many adults. Here are the steps to the exercise:

Discuss your child's nightmare with them and tell them you are going to help them deal with it - together.

Ask your child to lie down on their bed (familiar environment) and to close their eyes (though not always completely necessary). You can discuss the script before-hand especially if it is a really bad or recurring nightmare.

If you use script 2 or 3 make sure that you prepare the details thoroughly before you start. These scripts can be modified easily to suit your child's individual needs.

Script 1 - stopping the monster - you can run this through several times as a role play or game with toys or draw your own cartoons.

"Imagine that you are in the dream that scared you last night" (make sure you know what happened first)... *"Now, can you see me there with you? Right now it is you and me."* (Your child is now no longer alone but has an ally, you). *"Look, here comes the monster and it starts to chase us but it looks so funny and it is smiling. It has changed colour and it's like a rainbow... it sounds funny like a silly*

song... we both start to laugh... now it wants us to chase it... and the monster is now giggling... it is having fun... can you see me? I am just in front of you chasing the monster..." (We have begun to change the imagery, sounds and the monster's actions - this weakens the impact and fear factor)... *"Now stop everything... make everyone and everything in the dream freeze... we both put our hands up like a STOP sign... we both say to the monster in a very loud voice: 'Why are you chasing me and trying to make me scared of you?"* (Usually the monster or whatever it is will stop and answer). Then say: *"I don't like you scaring me anymore, I want you to change into something happy and start to be more friendly..."* (This usually turns out to be the end of the nightmare).

The process: Initiate memory of the nightmare / bad dream. Begin to change the imagery by making whatever the image is into something slightly different. Use variations of colour, size, position, character, sound and space to change the monster characteristics. Add yourself so that your child is no longer alone and engage yourself in the action as an ally and rescuer if need be. Usually adding something funny rapidly changes the tone of the dream. Stop the action - turn and confront the monster directly and tell it to stop scaring you both. You can even ask the monster what it wants and you may be quite surprised at its answers. Ask it to change into something happy. Practice playing with the new happy monster after it has transformed into something nice.

Script 2 - using a power ally

"Imagine that you are in the dream that scared you last night. You and your teddy bear," (or ten friendly but savage wolves, police squad, soldiers, yourself, whatever you both come up with that will be good allies in this fight against the monster). *"You are wearing a suit of armour, the sword of Truth, the shield of Honesty and a mini-machine gun just in case. Here comes the monster so let's scare the pants off it!"* (This aims to defuse fear and seriousness, it allows the human fight-response to operate and seems to relieve any feeling of dread and fear). *"Now freeze the monster in a block of ice. Ask the monster why it was trying to scare you last night. Tell it to behave itself in future or you'll be forced to frighten it again. In fact it could become your friend and protector when you go to sleep tonight but it first needs to change into something more heroic and beautiful, what did it change into?"*

You can also inject yourself into your child's imagery, as either their ally or as another companion.

Script 3 - guardian angels in bed - a variation of script 2

"Imagine that you are in the dream that you had last night. But this time your guardian, (which could be you, an angel, magician, Superman, Wonder Woman, Mum or Dad, Grandma or Grandpa), *is standing next to you and will be with you at all times when you go to bed at night. Here comes the monster, watch as your guardian*

protects you. Good, now you know that you can call upon them whenever you need to."

You can make many modifications to this theme. It takes time and practice to do this successfully. If you are creative enough and use your imagination you can tailor your child's dream imagery to suit the needs for each nightmare. Don't be afraid to ask your child what they think will work either. It might be the first thing you could try.

I always recommend that you practice this with your child for several weeks, every day, then every few days until it is a natural part of their bed routine.

Fantasy land - pain control for sick children

Children get sick a lot. In fact they can cause considerably more distress for the parents than for themselves. This simple exercise can be used to help harness the fertile potential of a child's mind. Talk to your child to discover what kind of fantasy world they would like to visit. Use their model for future imagery work. As an example for this exercise I will use the world of Narnia, from C.S.Lewis' series of books and movies.

"Imagine that you are in Narnia, just like the book that we are reading (or the movie). What can you see there?"

Now spend some time to embed your child in their fantasy world by walking them through some of the scenes, landscapes and meeting the characters. If there are any bad monsters around you can guide the fantasy to eliminate them according to the way your child wishes. Involve your child in creating a lovely healing environment over the next few minutes. Let them describe to you what they see and want to explore. This becomes your child's sanctuary. They can populate this sanctuary with any characters or real people they want.

"If you look around you will see a beautiful stream flowing slowly through the magical forest. Go over and put you hand in... it feels nice doesn't it? This stream is filled with magical water that has the power to heal any hurts or injuries anyone in the forest may have. Now scoop some water into your hand and taste it. Mmmm, delicious! You can actually feel the healing water starting to work on your illness" (whatever it is). *"Now splash your injury with the water. Feel it healing? You can even jump into the pool beside the stream because it is very shallow and safe. It looks like a small swimming pool for little children to heal themselves... Now you become very tired and you climb out of the pool. Together with your friends,"* (you can name them if there are any, or yourself if you are part of their imagery / inner world). *"You now dry yourselves on the nice warm towels resting on a branch. Put on the warm, clean clothes waiting for you. Look around until you find somewhere to rest,"* (hammock or similar, beds, couches, chairs, pillows, cushions). *"You and your friends now just want to go and have a nap or a sleep for a while... Now you are lying in the hammock and rocking from side to side, from side to side, from side to side... and as you start to fall asleep*

your body," (eczema, injury, disease, cold, sore throat, operation, sore thumb), *"begins to heal from the magical healing power of the stream and pool... the pain is slowly going and the magical forest / healer sends its healing energy to you as you swing from side to side in the hammock..."*

At about this time your child may be asleep or in a deep dream state.

You might also wish to include a magical healer in the fantasy like Aslan the lion from Narnia, Jesus, Buddha, teddy, the Power Rangers, Barbie, or whoever you and they think will fit in with your child's idea of a magical healer.

Bed wetting

There are many theories about the causes of bed wetting but we are focused on the cure. Guide your child to enter a nice fantasy world with the emphasis on awareness of when she has to go to empty her bladder. The alternative treatments include homoeopathy, herbs, vitamins, minerals, biofeedback, neurofeedback, acupuncture and an alarm that gets strapped to her back and goes off when wet. I have heard reports that the alarm works well (biofeedback) and neurofeedback can be quite successful too.

In their fantasy work suggestions of awareness are probably the best method for this form of treatment. When your child is involved with her fantasy world keep reminding them in a non-intrusive way that they are becoming more and more aware of the need to wake up and go to the toilet.

It is imperative that the environment remains positive and supportive - even though you may be feeling otherwise. Don't induce guilt or fear because it just makes things worse. It really doesn't work as bed wetting is caused by the neurological centres of the brain. It is very rarely a physical weakness.

Self-esteem can play a huge role in building a desire to engage in these fantasies too. Fear of punishment, guilt and humiliation are usually factors that need addressing as a result of being a bed wetter.

Aggression and embarrassment - the safe role of fantasy

Many problems can be played out in the safe environment of fantasy. If your child is being bullied at school she can get her own back in fantasy without harming anyone or getting into trouble in the real world. Fantasy is a safe environment to resolve and release stress and conflict.

In fantasy your child can replay any incident in which she was embarrassed or hurt. This time she can make it turn out the way she wants it to. She can even get her own back at those who hurt her. You can guide the fantasy to let go of the fear, embarrassment or whatever is causing her problems.

In my own practice this is a very useful technique for releasing frustration when in a powerless situation. Most issues resolve quickly after they have confronted their cruel teacher, school bully, boss, lover, mother, father, shop assistant or customer using fantasy.

Explain that this technique is OK when done under your supervision and in fantasy. It may not be appropriate to confront the school bully in real life but in fantasy it is safely done in a specific manner. Make a special time and place for fantasy work with your child. She'll respond with enthusiasm once she knows how easy it is.

One of my clients was a thirteen year old girl who used this with incredible results. Talia was alienated, isolated and completely friendless, an easy target for the school bullies. Within one week of fantasy work she had friends. Within two weeks the bullies were her friends too. One of them came over to her and shook her hand congratulating her on having some friends at last.

Resolving bullying through fantasy role play

Let me walk you through my work with a client to demonstrate how you can heal bullying.

One young man was bullied incessantly by his neighbours and the school bullies. One time his neighbours even let their dog attack him. Everyone including his brothers watched and laughed as this terrified little boy was attacked by the dog. He felt betrayed by his family, neighbours and everyone at school.

This client was gentle and shy - such an easy target for nasty kids - and kids can be very cruel. Thank goodness most of us grow up and make up for all the nasty things we did in our childhood.

After a few sessions we had established good rapport. As he began to trust me he opened up and told of the secrets he kept inside. Our hero had developed a severe scoliosis. He hated being tall and noticeable so he tried to shrink in height so that people wouldn't see him.

In a light relaxed state lying on the recliner in my office out came a little voice. There was a little boy inside him who couldn't understand why people were so cruel. This little boy who eventually had the name 'Thunder Cat' lived in his stomach. When stressed his stomach would knot and he would feel fear and nausea. This happened when meeting new people and even when just talking to friends and family.

In therapy he easily entered his deep psyche connecting with that part of him which manifested as pain, fear and nausea in his stomach. We had started down the road of healing to resolve one of his major problems - anxiety and panic and its resulting nausea.

It took several sessions talking to Thunder Cat to explain that he was not a bad boy. I explained that he had done nothing wrong to cause people to bully him. The nausea and anxiety began to ease. Then one by one out came other personalities: Gothic and Soldier, both had evolved to protect his fragile personality in times of suffering during his vulnerable teenage years.

I spoke to his personalities explaining that they had done no wrong that it was the bullies who were cruel. Each personality would talk and ask questions trying to understand why they felt this way. There were several minor personalities who arose at times but they disappeared as he healed.

Our hero had blamed himself for his mother nearly dying during his birth. He blamed himself for the cruelty of the kids at school. He blamed himself for everything that others had done to him.

His homework was to use the meditation CD I gave him to relax and heal. He particularly loved the 'castle' meditation where he had a dojo to train the inner boys in self defence. He created a whole supportive world, a sanctuary, right at his fingertips when he closed his eyes.

One of his exercises was to rescue himself as a small child. He did this by going into a traumatic memory from the past. He did this as his current self: an older, wiser, strong adult ready to defend his younger tortured self. He went to many traumatic memories that had caused so much suffering.

He would go into his fantasy world and beat up the bullies as he defended his little younger self. Time and again he went into his inner world until there was no more fear, to the point where the bullies would ask for forgiveness.

At one of our sessions he told me he had been woken by a dream. He said that the cheering woke him up and then he found himself witnessing his little self being a hero. He saw his younger self charging down a jousting lane as a knight in armour, lance in hand, knocking the bullies over left, right and centre. The crowd were cheering him. He said he could see the bullies piled together as he knocked them over one by one.

This fellow also had to learn to relax and so I taught him a powerful Taoist breathing meditation. He now goes to the gym, plays soccer and basketball where he is no longer afraid to challenge the ball. He is now becoming recognised as an outstanding player.

He still has a long way to go to fully consolidate these changes. There are times when he is still a little fragile but gone is the suicidal young man I saw at his first session.

Consolidation is an important stage in the tasks we seek to master. Practice makes perfect and inner practice is just as important as outer practice. I might also mention that we did a lot of neurofeedback training which helped settle his anxiety as well.

ANXIETY

Performing in front of an audience, public speaking, interviews or just going shopping can become a living nightmare for many of us. The more you think about it the more stressed you become and the more you seek to avoid the situation. Here are some scripts to assist with anxiety:

Stage fright - 3rd and 1st person - working backwards in time

Visualise yourself, 3rd person, performing live on stage, include close up visual images of yourself smiling and thoroughly enjoying yourself. Add sounds and comments of praise from others. Now enter the image 1st person and feel yourself achieving your goal. Add the feelings of pride, joy and excitement as you perform. Make the imagery as powerful as possible and it can have the effect of reducing anxiety.

Creating your future to the point that it actually occurs the way you have practiced is what we aim for. Perform this exercise every day in trance for several months before the event if possible. Practice again at least three times a day during the week before the event.

A variation is to start your visualisations of yourself in 3rd person as you walk out of the building at the end of the show. See yourself smiling and confident, excited and satisfied. Your unconscious will quickly realise that this means your performance went exactly and according to plan. Now work your way backwards in time to the performance itself. Working backwards is an extremely powerful technique that I have used successfully in my practice.

Interviews

Use the goal setting exercise and then imagine the interview setting and who will be there. Visualise yourself, 3rd person, relaxed and happy as you answer the questions honestly and easily. Imagine your interviewers just as relaxed and happy with your answers. Run through the interview several times making it powerful through the use of the 3 main senses (visual, feeling and sounds).

Always begin your meditations as early as possible giving yourself at least three to six practice sessions per day, one week prior to the interview. The more practice you do the less stressed you become and the easier it is when you get there. You can try working backwards with this as well.

Panic attacks

Panic attacks can be symptoms of deeper psychological issues. They can also be neurological in origin. For example a Vitamin B12 or Magnesium deficiency, for which I might suggest neurofeedback (a form of biofeedback) and nutritional supplementation. It is wise to do your research and speak to your medical professional before you try supplements. These two approaches are often quite successful in and of themselves.

Panic attacks manifest as shortness of breath, pains in the chest, tight throat, disturbed sleep, nervousness, agitation and other complaints particular to the individual. These symptoms may be caused by some underlying trauma from the past which is best dealt with in therapy by a qualified therapist.

Sometimes panic attacks are the result of an inherited predisposition to anxiety and they seem to come from nowhere. Childhood anxiety is very common, a genetic predisposition that leads to anxiety for no known reason and no known psychological trigger. The danger years for teenagers are from fifteen to twenty one years. This is when most suicidal thoughts and self harming starts.

When adults are exposed to long term stress, the stress hormones oxidise to become neurotoxins which damages the CNS (Central Nervous System - the brain). A myelin sheath surrounds each nerve and is composed primarily of cholesterol, an essential component of our nervous system. This nerve covering is easily damaged, which may explain why some people taking statin drugs (cholesterol lowering drugs) may experience muscle pain and nervousness after they have begun taking their statin medication.

A damaged myelin sheath, whether it be caused by stress-induced neurotoxins, physical brain trauma, an inherited weakness or from medication, results in many issues including anxiety and depression.

We know that there are many causes of anxiety and panic attack not all of them are psychological but a lot are. I have seen many kinds in my practice. All types have similar symptoms and are difficult to treat requiring individual and specific therapeutic approaches.

Mild levels of anxiety

By using the goal setting guidelines set out previously you can structure your self hypnosis to desensitise yourself from the source of anxiety. For example you could use the guidelines from the stage fright exercise. I also find that breathing for one or two minutes using a *'five seconds in and five seconds out'* cycle plus earthing techniques work well in managing anxiety. These exercises are discussed later in the book.

Exam nerves

It has often been said that the greatest cause of exam nerves is from failing to understand your material well enough. No amount of self hypnosis will help you if you do not put in the necessary study hours. Plan your study months before your exam and study regularly. I suggest using Mind Maps combined with self hypnosis, it worked for me. Incorporate your self hypnosis time into your study program with the following tips:

- Create your study environment as though it were the subject. Your room can have posters and objects reflecting the subjects you are currently studying. This acts as a subliminal reminder of the subject material. Plan your self hypnosis to enter the subject in a more tangible way - Einstein said that he came up with his ideas while in a dream or meditative state.

- Before the exam use your self hypnosis to imagine yourself in the exam room working easily on the exam paper. Create the setting, who else will be there, where you will sit, the supervisors and everything that goes with exams. Feel, see and hear yourself writing and answering the questions effortlessly. Use both 3rd and 1st person imagery.

- As you study you can create 'trigger words' associated with each subject. Do it by holding the material in your mind, in a light trance, and then squeezing your hand into a fist while saying something like *'Science!'*. Do this over and over, every time you study, until the trigger words and fist induce a massive recall of your *'science'* study material.

- If you forget your notes during a test or exam use self hypnosis. Firstly release tension as you exhale and say *'relax now'* three times. Next say your trigger words as you squeeze your hand into a fist. When you apply this combination your notes will pop into your head. If you practice this at every opportunity it will respond quickly and powerfully for you in the most stressful situations. Again, for this to work you will need to practice diligently.

The biggest problem with exams is nerves. By studying regularly you will be one step ahead, but add these other tricks and you can become a winner.

Fears and phobias - systematic desensitisation

If your phobia is so strong that you are debilitated by it then you may choose to see a therapist for specialist treatment. However you may want to try self hypnosis as well.

The most common method for treating many simple phobias is 'systematic desensitisation'. This is a process whereby you imagine the fear object at a distance then increase your image of it until it appears next to you. The next stage is to move from imagination into the real world. The real object is presented from afar and gradually it gets closer over a period of time. This process may take months to get this far, so don't rush it.

Previous methods will also work for you in specific anxious situations. I would add that you begin this approach in the 3rd person first. Once you are comfortable slowly introduce 1st person imagery.

Earthing - a technique for reducing stress

This exercise is very useful and very simple once you get the hang of it. We live with stress particularly with the eyes watching every movement and picking up subtle body language, ears straining to listen to the nuances of speech, throat tightening to hold back the words we often want to say, facial muscles tense portraying a calm and cheerful front, chest and heart muscles straining to hold back the tears of past hurts and stomach tense from anxiety and apprehension. This is a classic picture of the anxious person trying to remain balanced and in control.

We can contain so much tension that our body begins to form into strange shapes and muscles start to feel like they will stay that way forever. Our upper body demands more energy than the rest and can become congested. It can suffer the side effects in the manner of headaches, ulcers, heart attacks, throat problems and even sensory disorders.

By imagining your energy moving downwards into your feet you can effectively reduce tension in your upper body.

Step 1 - Earthing through feeling - an exercise from tai chi

Enter a light trance and imagine that your chi or life force is moving away from the stress points in your face, eyes, throat, chest and stomach and flowing downwards into your pelvis, legs and into your feet.

Step 2 - Soles of the Feet

Now imagine that your feet are radiating warmth from their soles like a heater. Become very aware of the sensation at the soles of your feet - this is critical.

Step 3 - Extending

If you are lying down in bed imagine that you can radiate energy from the soles of your feet as though your feet are stretching towards the wall opposite you or into the ground if you are sitting. Concentrate on the kinaesthetic or feeling sensations and as you breathe out imagine breathing any stress or tension out through your feet.

Step 4 - Earthing in times of stress

When confronted with stress take a deep breath and as you release it feel or imagine the stress leaving your body and entering the earth. Do this several times with your trigger words *'relax now'* until you feel relaxed, calm and clearer in your mind.

This exercise takes a lot of practice, but please don't be put off by that. This is also one of the most useful of all because with practice you will start to 'earth' tension automatically when in stressful situations. It is one of my favourite exercises from tai chi too.

WEIGHT LOSS, SMOKING AND RELATIONSHIPS

Hypnosis is seen as a panacea with the magical ability to make the user give up smoking or lose weight in just one or two visits. The reality is that hypnosis is not magic and you will have to make an effort to eliminate your bad habits. We not only develop unhealthy habits, we can also engage in unwholesome personal relationships. This chapter also explores some of the issues we face in establishing and maintaining our love relationships.

In the next few pages I will outline some simple techniques for you to try with some successful examples from my files.

Smoking

With the cost of cigarettes these days it's no wonder that people are trying to give up this habit. We use nicotine patches often waiting impatiently until the patch is off to have another cigarette. The habit easily becomes unconscious. We only realise we are smoking as we put the butt in the ash tray. Therefore the first step is to make the act conscious.

Script:

"Every time I reach for a cigarette I immediately become aware of what I am doing and I find it so easy to put the cigarette back in the packet. I then feel strong, successful and proud. Each day this

becomes easier and easier. I will not replace my smoking habit with any other destructive habit."

Next, imagine yourself in situations in which you would be tempted to smoke. Use the goal setting strategy outlined in this book, include using the 3rd and 1st person perspectives. For example, when having a drink with friends, after dinner, first thing in the morning. However this time see yourself as a non-smoker and loving it. Practicing your self hypnosis every day to reduce stress will also help. Replace the crutch with a habit that is more appropriate.

Not everyone will give up on the first try. In fact most will be smoking within nine months if they only attend the one session. The preferred method is to manage your improvement slowly, over three or four weeks, as your suggestions slowly sink in and work their way into your unconscious. Changing the habit from unconscious to conscious is the first big step though and the above script does that. Once you know what you are doing you have control – you can decide consciously whether to have that cigarette or not.

However, if there is a deep seated reason for why you smoke then you may need therapy to uncover it. I once had a client, Tim, who wanted to give up smoking but after each session he reported that he was smoking just as heavily - *"No changes, sorry"*.

Tim was a perfect subject, he went into trance easily and deeply each session. It puzzled me because this method had usually brought great success.

I decided that it was time to do some regression and I guided him to discover why he continued to smoke. He found that it was all because of his grandfather. Tim had never met his grandfather who died before he was born. His family, however, lovingly described his grandfather as a real man, a war hero, he could fix anything and he enjoyed a smoke. Tim's image was of this rugged, hero-type man with a cigarette in his hand leaning against the railing on the porch of an old house.

Tim's impression of himself was the same as that of his grandfather. A man's man. For Tim, giving up smoking meant that he would have to give up his belief that a man's man was also a smoker. He also had to accept that he wasn't his grandfather. After discovering why he had unconsciously resisted the suggestions to cease smoking, Tim was finally able to give up the habit.

Body shape and weight loss

Our physical appearance can influence the way we feel about ourselves. There are so many diets and weight loss programs that millions of trees have gone to the pulp mill to print them. In fact some dieters say that the food sold by companies for weight loss tastes like tree pulp too.

Our external appearance is sometimes considered a reflection of our inner state. What we present to the world is somehow linked to how we feel deep inside. It can also reflect our self-esteem and self-worth. Improve how we feel and we start to glow.

Why do models and movie stars get face lifts? How many people had a nose job and came out of their shell? In fact cosmetic, remedial surgery is now well accepted by the community to help improve a person's appearance.

Remember wanting to find a hole to drop into when you had pimples? When you are forced to appear less than your best you can feel judged, resentful, frustrated, humiliated and angry.

Hypnotherapy aims to change an unconscious habit into a conscious one. Then you have choices, for example to eat or not to eat. Using 3rd person imagery place yourself in the various situations where you would normally be tempted to over-eat or to eat fattening foods.

Next, imagine: see, feel and hear yourself maintaining self control and a healthy eating habit. Working on your self-esteem and self-worth may also need to be addressed in therapy. Firstly, we aim to turn an unconscious habit into a conscious one.

Script:

"Each time I reach for fattening foods or I'm tempted to overeat I immediately become aware of what I'm doing and find I can easily stop. I now crave slimming and healthy foods like fruit and salads. Each day I experience success and satisfaction in looking the way I want to look and feel the way I want to feel."

Now imagine yourself in situations in which you would normally be tempted to over-eat or to eat fattening foods. Imagine yourself being drawn irresistibly towards the healthy slimming foods instead and loving it.

Next imagine a figure of yourself, 3rd person again, looking and being exactly the way you wish to look and be. Wearing the clothes and acting just the way you want to. Using the 1st person mode imagine yourself inside that body and feel what it is like to be so assertive, confident, relaxed and slim. This is empowerment.

As in all inner work it is very important to do your goal setting first. Do the basics properly and you have a greater chance of success. Don't forget to examine your issues if they arise during these sessions. Many of my weight loss clients decide to resolve their emotional problems as part of their weight loss program.

Why do we over eat? Is love and acceptance a nice physical feeling? Is this comfort eating? Do you feel good when someone tells you they love you? Feeling good is a physical feeling and so is eating chocolate. There is a theory that we eat because it is a substitute for the affection and love that we are not getting in our lives. If this is the case then by resolving the affection problem you can resolve your weight problem.

One of my clients had to leave her husband before she was ready to move on to the next exciting stage of her life and achieve her goals. Her marriage had already gone beyond the point of no return before

I saw her. By going into those feelings of needing to eat and needing affection, she realised that there was more to this than losing weight.

Another client found herself eating the fridge empty after arguing with her husband over the phone.

When she hung up her friend asked: *"Why are you eating like that?"*

"Am I?" came her reply.

It didn't take long for her to realise why she binged out on food each time she argued with her husband. She was only trying to gain some comforting feelings from eating. It was also connected to the frustration of the life she was leading and being unable to express her anger.

Another client kept falling asleep during her self hypnosis sessions using my CD at home. She reported that she had lost 6 kilos (about 10 lbs) despite never finishing the first five minutes of the CD. She told me that she had this incredible craving for *'crisp, fresh salads'*. I was curious so we went through the CD and about three quarters through I say exactly those words: *'you find yourself craving crisp, fresh salads.'*

Losing weight or maintaining your desired weight is no easy thing to do. Approach it as a long term program, set your goals, elicit help from your loved ones and resolve the problems that deny you of love and affection.

Relationship problems - insight is the start of Delmore's healing

Delmore had never had a relationship. He wanted to be in a loving relationship with a woman but was terrified of them. Through therapy he uncovered a series of horrific childhood traumas where he had lost his confidence and sense of 'self' to dominant women. Actually, he didn't lose it, he had it taken from him.

Attending a religious school fifty years ago is not what it is today. Beatings happened each day and it was common practice for the nuns to humiliate their students in front of the entire school community as punishment.

Delmore had a very good friend at school, his name was Joey. Joey was undergoing chemotherapy for cancer and had lost his hair. He was the only child at school who was allowed to wear his hat in class. Joey wore his hat to cover the fact that beneath the hat he also wore a wig. His hair had fallen out and his mother didn't want him to feel different to the other students.

The young boys were so absorbed in their game of chasing that Delmore unconsciously snatched at Joey's hat. Off came the wig along with the hat and poor Joey started to cry. Delmore knew that he was now in deep trouble. He recalled from the morning's assembly that no one was to upset Joey.

He ran to the back of the playground quivering against the wire fence. He was already in a panic when running towards him he saw the playground teacher. The red-faced nun flew into a rage and beat

Delmore about the head repeatedly for his 'inconsiderate and cruel' act.

He was sent straight to Mother Superior's office. On his way there a nun asked why he was crying. When she heard what had happened she too started to beat the poor boy. By the time he made it to Mother Superior's office, Delmore was completely traumatised and distraught. He was barely able to tell her his sorry tale. When he had finished another bout of beatings began as Mother Superior raged, shouted and struck him repeatedly with her stick.

Placed outside Mother Superior's office the punishment continued throughout the day. At the end of lunch a special school assembly was called. Sobbing and retching, Delmore was forced to stand at the front of the school. Everyone witnessed another beating and several children cried as they watched the cane whipped at his bare legs again and again.

I tried my best to undo this traumatic history. In a light trance Delmore was guided to release the emotion locked inside. He was invited to go with the flow of his feelings, to strike out at the object of torture, even to swear or retaliate, if need be, to protect himself.

Delmore was powerless, impotent, his strength and power was stolen by the nuns all those years ago. A 1st person approach was impossible at this stage.

I next guided him to go to his younger self as he was now, as an adult, in 3rd person. He imagined that he went over to his little self standing alone at the front of the school assembly. He picked him up and hugged him and told him that he would protect him.

This was something that was much easier for him to do. Not once did he touch the nuns so strong was his fear of them. We ran through this many times - giving the little boy a hug and letting him cry in the safe arms of his older, adult self.

In his imagination, in a light trance, he spent months and years living with his family walking to school with his little, inner child. Staying with him at school day after day protecting him from the abuse of the nuns. There was not a single school day that Delmore left his inner child alone with them.

Delmore's problem was not sexual impotence he was attracted to women even though they had become the perpetrators of his emotional afflictions through physical and psychological torture and humiliation. This fatal attraction prevented him from forming and maintaining any close or long-standing relationships. It was hoped that with more therapy Delmore would be able to reprogram his mind to experience the joys of a close relationship with a woman.

As Delmore left he said that he had waited a long time to tell this story. Now that it is out the healing can begin.

Relationships - releasing the anger - 1st person

Another relationship problem was resolved quite quickly through therapy and self hypnosis. Todd was divorced, his wife left him because he couldn't communicate his feelings. Through regression he found himself being pushed into a cupboard by his grandmother. She forced him to stay in the cupboard all afternoon and into the night missing his evening meal.

This was the trauma that initiated Todd's inability to ask for help, to express himself when he felt trapped or defeated by life. He later found out that this happened quite often when he was sent to stay with his grandmother.

In a light trance he replayed the event in 1st person, he was really there. This time Todd refused to go into that dark and frightening place. We went over the incident again and again each time he became more assertive and eventually he pushed his grandmother away from him. He then ran outside to find his mother and father pulling up in their car.

In trance Todd was guided to see his father stand up for his son against this wicked grandmother. His father hugged him tightly to his chest which is a powerful healer in itself. He now felt safe and loved. Todd replayed these experiences at home in his own self hypnosis sessions over many weeks. That first week his family and workmates noticed the change in this once quiet and reserved young man. A year later Todd has since remarried and is in a wonderful relationship.

It's not always easy

Lucy married a man just like her father. He abused and treated her like dirt. She had two children before she left him. She then married a man just like her mother. Weak and depressed. He tried to commit suicide - she left him too. The third husband was just right, it was a bit like the three bears story.

When guided into trance to release her pent up emotions she was frozen. She was unable to even lift a hand against her father-in-law who had whipped her small son in front of her with a horse whip. She felt impotent. Her power was stolen first by her manic and cruel father, then by her first husband and then her violent father-in-law.

Now that she saw one of the pivotal traumas in her life when her son was whipped by her father-in-law, we could begin therapy. However, even in a light trance she couldn't face her father-in-law and we had to use other strategies. Sometimes when the front door is closed it is necessary to try a 'back door' strategy.

Over many sessions Lucy grew much more relaxed and she began to sort out her immediate life problems. She never did confront her initial trauma of seeing her son whipped. That event was always going to trip her up. However, the therapy we undertook for her self-esteem issues slowly eroded them down to a more manageable size. Lucy may seek further treatment if things turn bad but so far she is handling life with the aid of self hypnosis and her inner self meditations.

I recommend that you seek professional counseling in situations that have created severe trauma rather than try and deal with it in self hypnosis by yourself.

Inner healing with your inner child - a story with a happy ending

A young lady arrived for therapy one day and said she was trapped in her relationship and needed help. She said that she was having a nervous breakdown. The timid young lady sat opposite me and I was worried that she might not have the strength even for therapy. She told me of her nasty boyfriend who beat her with his leather belt; her boss who took advantage of her mercilessly; and her broken-down wreck of a car that her boyfriend had found for her.

I thought to myself, *"How can I help her find the strength to work through this terror and pain?"*

I knew that it had to come from within. I was responsible to help her find the courage and strength to change her life. I should be able to find a way - this is what I do isn't it? My brain went into overdrive to come up with a suitable therapeutic approach.

I asked her to close her eyes, relax and imagine she could go inside her psyche and find her 'inner child'. She was quiet for a time and then she said, "*I can see a little girl in the forest, it's me, it's me when I was about five years old.*"

By this time it was the end of the session and we had run out of time. I told her to visit this little girl every night and get to know her.

A week later I saw her and asked, *"How did your inner work go, how is that little girl now?"*

She replied that it was useless.

'Oh boy," I thought to myself, *"this is not good.'*

This process has never failed me and I was not about to let it fail now.

"Tell me, what happened when you did your inner work at home?" I asked.

She replied, *"Every time I went inside to find her I would see her playing in the forest. I would go up to her, you know, to get to know her, to be her friend, but she would then run away. So I gave up, it's useless, she doesn't even want to know me. I feel that even my inner child has rejected me, everyone in my life abandons me."*

I was a bit upset myself I had given her homework to do that she hadn't been properly prepared for. I felt that I had failed her too. 'But,' I thought, *'I know what to do now.'*

"OK, I think I know what's going on and I think I know how to fix it," I said.

She smiled at me and I was amazed at the trust she placed in my ability to help her. She closed her eyes and slowly relaxed and slid into her unconscious world. I told her to find that little girl and if she ran away she was to chase her. No matter where that little girl ran she was to chase her and NOT give up until she had caught her.

After a few minutes her face turned serene, calm and her breathing slowed. I could tell that she was in a nice place. Then slowly with a smile on her face she opened her eyes.

"You know that little girl? That was me. Did you know that my mother died giving birth to me? My mother died when I was born and I thought that I had killed her. Even though I was a baby I knew my mother died, I could feel it. I felt that she had abandoned me, left me. I hadn't realised that until now. I was then taken to live with my grandmother, my mum's mother, she was such a lovely old lady. But she died when I was only 2 years old. I thought that I killed her too. She was the second one I cared for that abandoned me. When my grandmother died I had to live with my father and his stupid wife, the 'wicked step-mother'. She eventually kicked me out when I was 13 years old. I didn't even know it but I have lived with this sense of loss, abandonment and guilt all my life."

I sat back in my chair. I was crying as she told me her story. The timid young lady continued:

"I was so afraid to lose anyone. My boyfriend is a monster, I hate him, he beats me but I stay with him because I'm afraid to lose him. I have lost all the people I love and I always thought that it was my fault. Today I discovered that little girl inside me, but even she ran away from me. She abandoned me like my mother, then my grandmother and finally my step-mother. They all abandoned me, every one of them, even my useless father abandoned me.

"I remember waking up in the forest and you telling me not to stop, that I had to keep chasing my little self and not to let her get away. So I did. I chased that little girl. She didn't run very far when she stopped and I caught her. She smiled up at me and I knew, I knew everything. I knew that I didn't kill my mother, I didn't kill my grandmother. I realised that the little girl wanted me to prove to her, that, unlike my mother, unlike my grandmother, and unlike my step-mother and father, I would NOT abandon her.

"So she stopped when I had proven that I wouldn't abandon her and that was what I was meant to do. I had to prove that I would stay with her, something that none of my parents had done for me. And then I realised that they never did abandon me. My mother died and grandma died because that's what happens in life. I knew that the moment my little girl stopped and let me catch her. And then I realised that no one has ever abandoned me, life is just like that. The little me smiled and let me hug her. I proved to her that I would NEVER abandon her, ever."

The next time I saw her she had dumped the loser boyfriend and moved out. She had a new job where she was valued and she had even bought a new car.

Sometimes we need to go inside our psyche to find the truth of our existence. This young lady did just that, she found her Truth and then she found the strength to change. It is such a simple technique but an incredibly profound one. It is so profound that I will be writing another book on the 'inner child therapy' some time in the future.

AGE REGRESSION

We are essentially emotional beings. Our past is often littered with events that have left deep emotional scars. Just imagine something happening that was so frightful that you become traumatised each time you are reminded of it. To prevent the trauma from resurfacing we push it deeply into our unconscious until we eventually forget that it had even occurred. Freud called this automatic response to trauma, 'repression'. These traumatic memories are known as 'repressed memories' which form the foundations for many of our psychological problems.

In regression therapy we accept the images or experiences that arise and have a negative impact on the client. We therefore approach therapy with these 'repressed memories' in much the same manner as we would a remembered trauma. I have always explained to my client that a repressed memory may or may not have really occurred.

There remains considerable debate regarding repressed memory in psychology circles. Unless you were there to witness the event yourself you will never know for sure if what your client recalls was a real event or not. Psychotherapists accept that regardless of whether the memory is real or not, we will always provide our client with the most appropriate therapy at our disposal.

As professionals we apply Dr Carl Rogers' foundational tenet of 'unconditional positive regard' - remaining non-judgmental, empathic and professional in accepting our client at where they are on their journey of healing. Our role is not to judge but to provide the best treatment and therapeutic environment to guide our client to heal. We do that by practicing therapy regardless of our personal beliefs.

Your unconscious contains certain drives, urges and instincts that have been bothering it for years, much like a thorn in your foot. The thorn festers so badly that you can become handicapped by it. You put up with the discomfort because it is too frightening to look too deeply into your unconscious to resolve it. While in trance your unconscious can begin to release this trauma that has been screaming for your conscious attention.

Regressing to a traumatic incident is likened to removing the festering thorn. The next stage of therapy is to clean the wound while the last stage is to learn to walk properly again.

On the odd occasion you may re-experience symptoms of your past. One lady I worked with regressed back to when she was five years of age. Towards the end of the session she began scratching. When she awoke she just couldn't understand why she felt so itchy. Then she realised that when she was five she had a bad dose of measles and had missed two weeks of school.

The images that present in trance have some bearing on what is troubling us. Look at them but don't get too carried away trying to analyse them. Jung suggested we look at these trance experiences over a period of time until we eventually discover what they mean.

One dream or trance experience may take months to understand. Jung himself stated that a particular dream took him years of analysis before he discovered what it meant.

I don't want you to think that all of your problems can be set at the feet of your parents either. Being a good parent is one of the hardest challenges in life. We all make mistakes by commission and omission (doing and not doing). If you discover a problem from childhood deal with it responsibly don't seek to lay blame or to get revenge, this is not healing. If things are that bad seek professional counselling.

It is also possible that we bring many of our problems into this life and they manifest regardless of the best intentions of our parents and our caregivers.

Please note that you will rarely take on the voice, mannerisms and mentality of an earlier age. This looks good in the movies and on the stage but it is rare, however some super-suggestible people can regress to that level.

Childhood trauma - reprogramming the past - 1st person

Twenty five year old Sylvester came for therapy to treat his severe panic attacks. He had first visited a psychiatrist who explained that his symptoms suggested that he was experiencing panic attacks. This insight was his first step to recovery but the anti-anxiety drugs he was prescribed were not helping.

Sylvester went into trance easily and at his 3rd session he regressed spontaneously back to a car accident when he was four years old. He experienced the distress of being taken by a well meaning woman and carried away from the scene of the accident. He heard the panic in a bystander's voice, *"Get the child away!"*

He remembers his blood covered mother lying unconscious in the front seat of the car. When his father took him to visit her in hospital she was wrapped in bandages, she was lying very still. Her eyes were closed, death-like. He wouldn't go into her room, that wasn't his mother.

The fear, loneliness and extreme trauma of being helpless and finding himself in a hopeless situation created the first link in the chain towards a predisposition for anxiety.

The regression was quite traumatic for Sylvester. He was really there. Now that we knew what had initiated his panic attacks we needed a suitable therapy to begin his healing.

Sylvester was guided back to the car immediately after the accident. He was then guided to see his father climb out of the car and tell the woman to leave his son alone. His father then picked Sylvester up in his strong loving arms and held Sylvester so very tight and told him it was all going to be fine. Sylvester can't remember his father ever holding him. This in itself was a very powerful emotional experience.

Next, Sylvester's father opened the door to where his mother was seated. His father wiped the blood off her face. I said, *"Look, she's opening her eyes, her face is clear, she calls your name and puts her hand out for you, take it, she holds you in her arms now."* The therapy continued as Sylvester quietly sobbed with relief.

He was then guided into the hospital to where the next link in the chain of anxiety was created. He saw his mother in bed asleep. I said, *"Look, there's your mother, she's asleep."*

"She looks like she's dead," came his wooden reply.

I then said, *"She opens her eyes and calls you over, you rush to her side and she looks fine - there's no blood, no injuries. She is now holding you so tightly, feel her arms holding you."*

By this time Sylvester is sobbing again. He is completely involved with the events as they unfold.

The sobbing was not of sorrow or fear but one of release of anxiety, isolation, separation and of love. If you can remember what it was like to be held by your mother or father in a time of trauma, then you will know what it was like for Sylvester. What a beautiful feeling of security, to be safely protected from the terrors of the world.

By the end of the session Sylvester was quite exhausted but relieved. He experienced a traumatic incident in a new light that, with practice, will slowly replace the old one. Remember that our memory is not infallible it recalls whatever experience it thinks it had. In this case it was now digesting the new 'safe' car accident.

The technical term 'abreaction' or 'catharsis' is the release of pent up emotional tension. At the end of the session Sylvester shook from head to toe from the release of twenty years of emotional trauma.

Sylvester called me a few days later. *"I couldn't wait until our next appointment,"* he said, *"I just wanted to tell you that I think I am cured. I haven't had a panic attack since the last session."*

I told him that his news had made my day.

"You've made my decade!" was Sylvester's reply.

Sylvester is still working with self hypnosis and is completely over his anxiety.

Some inter-generational insight

A young lady, Sally, came for help to lose weight. She regressed spontaneously back to recall a number of incidents in her early childhood, these were verified by her mother the following week. However the big event was when she regressed back to a very strange incident.

"I am seeing a child being made ready for a bath," Sally said.

"Who is it?" I asked.

"It isn't me... it's my mother, she is about 5 years old... I don't like it here, I want to get out..." Sally was starting to get distressed so I brought her out of trance.

That week she saw her mother and at the next session Sally related this story.

When her mother was five years old her elder brother and sister put her into the bath with her baby brother. The two older children were doing their parents a favour by bathing the youngsters. But the little boy who had been very sickly from birth, drowned in the bath. Now this was a family secret no one ever spoke about, ever. Sally had no way of knowing this.

Somehow Sally had tapped into her mother's childhood through the trance state. Was this incident related to why she couldn't lose weight? It appears so. The trauma that the mother suffered by witnessing her brother drowning and the ensuring events may have created the beginning of Sally's problem. Since these sessions Sally has now been able to lose her excess weight and to keep it off these past two years.

Anxiety is often caused by stressful childhood incidents. Going back to rescue your younger self, and then reliving it the way you want it to have happened, can be a very rewarding exercise. However I always recommend that you seek the aid of a skilled therapist. Dwelling on negative past experiences is not healing, it is not therapy. It is the active changing of events and reliving the new happier ones that can be therapeutic.

Many woman and men have been sexually assaulted in childhood. This has also responded to trance therapy. However, I implore you to seek professional support if you have experienced childhood abuse or trauma.

I've lost my daddy

This case study helps illustrate how our memories never really disappear over time. Laura was seventy years old when she decided to seek therapy for her inability to form close, loving relationships. After an hour of history taking and discussing her past I discovered that when she was eight years of age her father disappeared. Her mother said that daddy would be home one day but that day never arrived. Every day she would run out into the streets looking for her daddy. She would sometimes see a man walking down the street towards her house, but it was never her father.

For over sixty years Laura grieved the loss of her dear father. It was a constant grief that dogged her life with sadness. In therapy I guided her to go back to that eight year old and hug her, to talk to her and to win her trust.

Over the next two sessions Laura sat with her younger self, then her 18 year old followed by other selves of various ages, hugging and talking, explaining to her inner selves how life moves on. The changes I witnessed in her through this process reinforced that the therapy I was using was completely appropriate.

At our last session she went to heaven to meet her father. There were tears of joy and some of sadness. By the end of her therapy this beautiful lady was able to place her life into perspective and each night she would visit her inner selves for a chat and a hug.

Laura stopped seeing her father on TV, on the street and in the shopping mall. She began forming relationships with others in her neighbourhood and finally found a partner she could love.

The detective - lost and found

Gail came for help to find some lost money. She had just held a party where someone presents things for sale and your friends come along and buy them. Gail had collected $500 from her friends over the past few weeks and was ready to pay for their goods. But she had forgotten where she'd left the envelope with the cash. The day she was to pay for the goods she had a visit from a friend. After her friend left she found that the money was missing. Gail was certain that she had left the money on top of the fridge but it was now gone. Not wanting to blame a good friend she went for help.

After some time in trance she kept coming back to putting the $500 on the fridge but was unable to go any further. She was starting to feel stuck, fixated on the money on top of her fridge. I thought that she could do with a different perspective. So I guided her to seek help from the Sun archetype. I have always found this to be useful in stuck situations like this.

The Sun showed her what had happened on a movie screen in her mind. Gail saw herself in her kitchen having a cup of tea with her friend. She then saw herself standing to go to the bathroom. While she was gone her friend quickly scanned the kitchen and found the envelope containing the $500. Her friend than placed the envelope into her handbag.

The technique I used was to regress Gail back to the last time she remembered putting her envelope down. I guided her to follow the action from there. I brought in the Sun archetype when I thought that she was becoming frustrated and stuck, it worked. Her friend did own up to the theft but to this day has never returned the money.

Memory lane

One thing you can do if you want to practice regression is to allow yourself to recall pleasant memories in trance. Memories of childhood are not all bad there are plenty of great times locked in that big unconscious vault. You can go back in time and enjoy them again. It is like walking down memory lane and it should be quite enjoyable.

For the older readers you can recall your loves all those years ago. Recalling past lovers and the fun times you had together is a more constructive past-time than recalling negative memories. Practice your goal setting and involve all five senses.

Interestingly, doing this form of inner child therapy will lead you to have dreams and memories of childhood. The interesting part is that these dreams and memories are not negative or traumatic at all. I've seen this happen time and again and now accept that healing the past leads to a happier and healthier now.

Repressed memory - can be a problem

A word of warning. Don't take everything you uncover in trance as real. Our memories may take on an event from a conversation, book or movie that you relate to on some level. If you recall a trauma it could be a combination of real events, a conversation you overheard, a book or two and a few movies all mixed together.

Point of view is another thing to consider in repressed memory. One story I heard was about a woman who had panic attacks every time she saw cows. When this lady was two years of age her parents had a picnic by the river right next to where some cows were grazing. To her horror one of the cows sat on her.

Through regression she discovered herself staring at these huge frightening creatures - the cows. At that exact moment her puppy came racing over and jumped on her. The poor child was so absorbed in these monstrous cows that the physical trauma was fixed by her visual memory of the cows. From that moment, until she undertook therapy, she was afraid of cows. Once she understood that it was her dog and not the cows, she was able to heal.

Past Life Rescue at a Healers Clinic

I was once sitting in a healers waiting room looking forward to a wonderful healing session. To my surprise the healer came into the waiting room with a worried frown on her face and said, *"I need you to come into my room and help this lady. Spirit told me that you would be able to help her."*

I went into her tiny healing room and there on the massage table was a lady of middle age. She was crying and babbling in a strange child-like voice. I leaned forward and asked her to tell me what was happening. She stopped crying and said that she was being burned at the stake. She was a little girl and it was hurting. The little girl felt frightened and was in considerable pain from the flames. She tried to describe the smoke and flames but then began crying again.

I immediately guided her firmly to step out of her body and to look at the little girl. I explained that this was herself from a past life. The woman followed my instructions and again began to cry, but this time of sorrow, sadness and compassion. I asked her to go back in time a little to when the girl was not burning at the stake. She could easily do this.

As she began to relax I guided her to go to that little girl and to hug her, to take her away to a safe place, a sanctuary, and to nurture her just like a mother would. This lady then started to change her past life trauma. With me guiding her, she next took the little girl into the future to live with her, and thus began another adventure in this lifetime. Yes, our inner world is an amazing place.

SPORTS HYPNOSIS - MENTAL REHEARSALS

In the elite sports category the difference between good and great can appear to be insurmountable. Most of an athlete's performance relies on their mental state on the day of competition. Accordingly, self hypnosis is part of their training schedule. Research into sports and successful athletes concludes that mental imagery is one of the keys to their success.

Successful athletes will 'imagine' their performance before competing using the 3rd person / 1st person perspective outlined in the goal setting chapter. By going into the trance state and creating your best performance you set up neural pathways to ease that performance into reality.

Professional sports is an enormous money making industry and every elite athlete wants to claim their place at the very top. Money and fame are there to be had if you can put in that extra oomph and leap into this elite category. Many athletes may be rated as good but it is the elite athlete that draws upon extra reserves of strength and determination to cut the edge every time. If you devoted thirty minutes each day to mental rehearsals then you too can become one of this special group.

Sports hypnosis is such a huge field that all I can hope to do here is introduce you to some of its key concepts. To whet your appetite, please read on.

Only last week one of my clients, a teenage footballer, had his best game in two years after a single session where he was taught mental rehearsals. Everyone knew he had it in him, his challenge now is to continue with his mental rehearsals to maintain this top level performance. One day he could be offered million dollar contracts too.

One of my first clients was one of Australia's top triathletes. Terry was already an Australian Champion at that time but was suffering from pre-competition stress. With some tuition he quickly learned to use mental rehearsals in his deep trance meditations as part of his training schedule. Those personal qualities that earned him the status of an elite athlete ensured that he would use these exercises to achieve even greater success.

In a very short time Terry was back on top as he traveled to Canada and the US to compete in their championships and then the World Triathlon competition. That year Terry won five out of the six French National Triathlon Championships. In the 6th race he was pipped at the post by a half second.

The Australian 'Fosters Ironman Triathlon' is so exhausting and damaging to the competitors that they are often unable to train for up to three months after the event. The race lasts for nine and a half hours, for the open speedsters, and about fifteen hours for the older and less experienced. It is a 5 km swim, 180 km bike ride and 42 km run, one after the other without a break. Terry used the trance state to bring his mind, body and spirit into alignment. He programmed every cell to co-operate with each other before, during and after the event.

Terry prepared for four months prior to the race. His mental rehearsals included visualisations of the entire race where he emphasised how his body would handle the stresses of this massive physical and psychological challenge. He programmed himself to finish with energy in reserve with no injuries and that his entire body would co-operate to reduce lactic acid build-up and to repair tissue damage.

At forty-five-years of age Terry was now in the Veteran Class. He finished seven minutes behind the twenty eight year old world champion; swam his personal best; his bike leg was perfect; he finished nineteen minutes ahead of his career best time.

Terry finished the race in a 2 km sprint. When he entered the medical tent to sign off at the end of the race, the race physician performed the regulation blood pressure test. The doctor looked at his blood pressure and declared that Terry wasn't one of the competitors and shouldn't even be in the medical tent. Fortunately one of the nurses had seen Terry sprint in and came to his rescue. She told the doctor that he had indeed competed, the doctor was amazed. Twenty five percent of all competitors were put on drips after the event.

All competitors travel with a driver because they aren't able to move the next day. Terry drove home, for the next eight hours his driver remained in the passenger's seat. On the way out of town he stopped to let one of the TV hero 'ironmen' cross the road. The poor guy wasn't able to raise his head to say hello. He even had to use his hands to lift his legs over the curb.

Attributes common to elite athletes

- *Goal setting* – they set short and long term goals that are realistic and achievable. Goal setting increases concentration and focus by over 50%. They use goals for each training session and in competition.

- *Beliefs* - they believe that there are no limits, their self image is high. They believe that they will achieve their goals.

- *Modelling* - they model or copy the training schedules and performance of the most successful athletes in their field.

- *Mental Rehearsals* - they rehearse their performance repeatedly in a light trance state as described in this book. This is the single most powerful exercise used. It is as important as physical training. It is vital when the athlete is unable to physically train through poor weather, off season and injury.

- *Stress management* - before and during competition. The ability to focus immediately before competing and to regain composure after a set back is directly related to practicing stress management techniques.

- *Concentration* - elite athletes are able to perform consistently at their peak by maintaining concentration at critical times. Most performance problems are due to negative self talk. They learn thought-stopping techniques and substitute them with positive arousal states.

- *Control* - an athlete may have the criteria for optimum performance but without self-control they may not be able to call upon those skills successfully when needed. Self control is an essential quality of the elite athlete.

- *Commitment and drive* – they practice every day, even on Christmas Day. They well understand that without commitment they will gain minimal success.

- *Performance arousal* – they train to boost their energy levels at critical moments which helps increase arousal and focus. Elite athletes can call upon reserves of energy long after most have given up.

- *Gaining the edge* – they study their opponents for weaknesses and strengths then develop strategies to win. They warm-up alone or with their coach prior to competition. They will seek a quiet location to visualise their perfect performance and to centre emotionally and physically. Research has shown that the few minutes before competing are vital in creating optimum performance.

- *Recovery* - top athletes recover rapidly by caring for their mind, body and spirit. They have a massage, spa, sauna, shiatsu, etc. when they need it. They will allow themselves a few moments to cry or sulk after losing before they get back into training for the next competition. Elite athlete use the services of sports psychologists and therapists to improve their performance and thus gain the edge over their opponents who don't.

In summary, prior to each training session write down your goals then imagine yourself achieving them – this is what is called 'mental rehearsal'. Create a state that includes physical and emotional arousal and believe in yourself.

Many top athletes find that they hit low spots in their performance when personal relationships are falling apart. If this occurs seek immediate therapy before you fall in a heap at the bottom of the ladder.

Martial arts

The martial artist undertakes decades of disciplined training and meditation to become a master. It must be understood that the explosive kicks and punches of boxing, karate and tae kwon-do often require different mental rehearsals to those that train the internal force of kung-fu and tai chi.

Force is developed through physical training to strengthen the muscles and skeletal structures. By applying self hypnosis to your forms, kicks and punches you can increase power and accuracy. Training would follow the same mental rehearsal exercises of any other sport. Physical centering is another aspect that is essential in the martial arts.

Centering is a technique of placing your awareness on an area of the body called the 'Tan Tien' in Chinese; it is called the Centre Point in English; in Japan it's called the Hara. This is at or just below the navel and resting just inside the abdomen. Imagine it as a tight, bright and glowing ball of light. Sometimes you can physically tighten your abdominal muscles to stimulate it. Imagine that you can breathe in and out of the Tan Tien then feel it become your centre of physical power.

The Tan Tien is cultivated over many years and was one of the great secrets of the martial arts families of China, Korea and Japan. Today the wisdom of the ancient martial arts is freely available. We have Bruce Lee and many others to thank for this knowledge.

The internal power of kung-fu and tai chi is achieved through the dedicated practice of centering and their slow moving patterns or forms. The aligning of the physical with the mental and spiritual bodies is the goal of this form of internal training. When you become aware of your chi or energy flowing through your body, you will be ready to practice the more spiritual aspects of martial arts.

At the highest level there is no combat, no confrontation, complete non-resistance as your opponent will be unable to touch you. This was demonstrated by my tai chi master, Simon Lim, when he asked us to try and kick him during one of our lessons. Simon intuited where we would move before we even moved. His control of his personal space was so complete that we couldn't touch him. No matter how hard we kicked we still fell over.

Arousal states

Anthony Robbins, in his book on NLP, 'Unlimited Power', suggests this exercise. While in the trance state recall any moments in which you felt proud, successful and a real winner. Take one of these memories, or imagine one if you can't, and create it using the 3rd and 1st person perspectives.

When in the 1st person perspective create this feeling of being a winner. Make it so strong that you are really there breathing and feeling the ripples of pleasure of winning. Now at the peak of this 'high' clench your right fist into a tight ball and say 'Yes!' to yourself. Repeat this six times until you feel so powerful that nothing will stop you from achieving your goal.

Repeat this exercise every time you do something successful. This winning or arousal state is a powerful way to create a winning edge during competition. This is especially useful in sports that require bursts of speed or aggression. For more relaxed sports like golf it can still be applied but modify it to one of focus, control and relaxation. Golf is a specialist sport like tennis requiring control, stamina and correct positioning of the body without conscious awareness. This includes the reflex action of the volley and the smooth follow-through of the golf swing.

In golf use visualisations for every shot as though it were the only one. Mentally rehearse the ball going exactly where you want it. The same as for tennis. Play each shot as if it were the only one and follow the guidelines outlined earlier.

Ballroom dancing is not usually seen as a competitive sport until you talk to someone training for competition. Neil is a young man using self hypnosis to become a professional ballroom dancer hoping to start his own dance studio.

He is not the perfect athlete and drives me to distraction by staying up late every night, falling asleep during his trance sessions and not conforming to the guidelines set out in the last few pages. However Neil has natural ability that has been brought to the fore through consistent mental rehearsals visualising his performances.

Now that he is in the adult grades competing as a 16 year old against the elite is no mean feat. Last week he came 2nd in a state competition against the professionals. He no longer becomes nervous because he has learned the value of finding a quiet place to do his pre-competition mental rehearsals.

When I ask if he has been doing his daily exercises, Neil answers, "*I like to be with others, I'm a social person.*" He has developed nerves of steel and feels bullet proof like most teenagers.

You too can get to the top if you follow the simple guidelines outlined in this chapter. Word is out that sports hypnosis works and novices use it as a means to improve their performance in their drive to become elite athletes.

MEMORY, STUDY, CREATIVITY AND DREAMING

Anyone can have a lapse of memory. From the scatter-brained professor, the hormonal teenager, the overworked and stressed parent to the senility of old age we can have it and lose it at any time. It is believed that we only use about 1% of our mental potential. If we doubled our thinking power then we are still only using 2%. Self hypnosis will help you expand your intellectual potential but as you will see you have to put some effort into your mental rehearsals first.

If you have a poor memory and want to improve your recall then make your object or subject extremely memorable. If you recall in the earlier chapters our mind talks using all five senses. By applying the strategy of thinking in images, sounds, feelings, smells and tastes you will certainly improve your memory.

Study

To recall something important, try to first program it the way the subconscious processes and stores it. The brain does this primarily using the three main senses: images, feelings and sounds. Educator and author Tony Buzan, explains that we remember something that is novel or amusing. In other words try to make your imagery unusual and if you can, add humour. We remember most what we hear or read first and last so make your study sessions short and often. We remember best what we have just learned: so make notes within ten minutes of a lesson - before you forget it.

By reviewing your lists or notes regularly over the following few days, you will find that it is absorbed into long-term memory much quicker. Basically this translates as 'practice' until you know it thoroughly.

For those who have found they need to study harder than everyone else you'll find strategies that will give you the edge. Self hypnosis can also aid to reduce exam nerves and provide the right atmosphere for your study.

One simple rule to remember: if you don't have the information in your head in the first place no amount of trance work will put it there. Do your formal study first.

A learning environment

One technique for your study is to create an atmosphere specific to the subject that you wish to learn. You can place objects such as posters, lists, key words and artifacts of your subject around your study room. Read your notes in that environment. Then, using self hypnosis, enter a light trance and imagine that you are 'at one' with your subject. Understanding your subject is more than reciting lists: it is a holistic state leading to mastery.

Anchoring memory triggers using humour and novelty

If you want to remember day to day things then you can create those unusual, novel images. If, for instance, you wish to remember to phone a friend when you get home tonight try this: visualise an image of your friend with a cartoon head squeezing out of your phone - now fix that image to your door knob.

By making the image clear and bright, full colour, and funny - by hearing your friend giggling as she tries to get out of the ear piece, you will recall this series of images and sounds when you reach for the door knob. If you practice this image several times during the day you won't forget it when you reach home.

In summary this method uses our knowledge of how the mind works, the five senses. This is triggered when anchored to a physical object using novelty and humour.

Novelty stimulates the mind

A powerful phenomenon of memory is novelty. If it is interesting and stimulating then you will remember it. A friend needed to recall the details of specific aircraft parts for an engineering exam. He was strongly motivated and had previously used this technique of novelty and humour as a young man. He found to his surprise that he was able to recall parts and statistics learned years before. He did this by using funny faces, cartoons and the sounds of laughter specific for each item.

If your day to day life is boring and uneventful then it is common to struggle to recall recent events. This is the problem of the elderly: they remember the past easily because they have practiced remembering it over many years. However, when they try to remember what they did yesterday they often fail.

Automatic writing for high distinctions at university

I will give you an example of how I survived university with three children, a broken down car, a mortgage and working three jobs. I forced myself to study hard, long hours to fill my mind with the material I needed for my essays. I would then lie down on my bed with a note pad and a pen in my hand. As soon as my head hit the pillow the essay or assignment would start to form in my mind. Complete sentences and even full paragraphs were there ready for me to write down. I would sit up and begin writing as the words came to me. I wrote most of my essays this way.

In preparation for exams I would create page after page of Mind Maps for each subject (please read Tony Buzan for more information on this incredible study method). Part of the process of using mind maps is to visualise and engage unconsciously with them in preparation for exams. Through the deliberate and dedicated practice of meditating on these mind maps I was able to complete my exams in almost half the time as the other students. Often I was the first out of the exam room. I am not smarter than anyone else and I admit that I have to work extremely hard to master any subject

I am interested in. This method of study and meditation made the difference between a pass and high distinctions.

Creativity - right brain, trance and dreams

You can create your next masterpiece by stimulating your creativity and allowing it to gestate using your self hypnosis exercises. Opening up to the creative side of your brain is one of the many uses of self hypnosis. We now know that the unconscious mind operates by using the five senses with an emphasis on the top three: visual, auditory and kinesthetic or feeling senses.

Artist, Anthony Jones, uses this technique for his brilliant works. Firstly he explores the various concepts contained in the book he is about to illustrate. He then researches various images and ideas that begin forming in his mind. He then becomes totally immersed in the project through gestating these images, sensations and concepts. Next he sleeps on it until he intuitively knows what the cover will look like. Anthony would often wake up in the middle of the night or early morning with the images fully formed.

By immersing your conscious mind in the topic you wish to create you allow your unconscious to work at its own pace and in its own way. How many people have a midday nap and wake up with the answer to a problem? Albert Einstein, Thomas Edison and even Salvador Dali credited their creativity and inspiration on their daily power-naps.

To relate from personal experience: when I write an article, a blog or book chapter, I use self hypnosis to relieve the strain of being at my computer for hours each day. During these sessions I will often unconsciously review what I have written and come up with a better version or new inspiration. I would simply lie on my bed with pen in hand and note book beside me. Once my head hits the pillow, sentences and paragraphs would form in my mind and I would sit up and write them down.

I made it through university by using self hypnosis. My best projects have benefited from these short power-naps. Many of the exercises in this book have come to me whilst in trance. I believe that these power-naps, trance and dreaming states are the most natural creative states available to us.

Bubbles

The bubble method is what I sometimes use in my clinical practice to help clients gain inspiration and insight. Enter a light trance and imagine several large, clear bubbles floating in front of you. Contained in these bubbles are ideas, images, feelings, messages or whatever it is you wish to work on. Make sure that you do your goal setting to program your unconscious on what it is you wish to explore and create.

This method is great for harnessing the power of your unconscious and directing it to work on specific issues in the background while you get on with living. For example you may have problems with your relationship. Create a bubble and place the issue inside. Direct your unconscious to resolve it and to come up with inspiration in your dreams and meditations. Then let it go remembering to practice every day until you gain insight. This allows your unconscious to work uninhibited and uninterrupted by your conscious mind.

Dream incubation - put it in and let it go

Begin your dream programming by first creating your goals and then thoroughly immersing yourself in the material necessary for your project before going to bed. The intention is then stored in your unconscious. Do not try or force it just put it in and let it go. If you wake during the night you can reaffirm your intention and then let it go again. Do not dwell on it. When you wake up try to write down what came to you in your dreams. Not every session will produce a brainstorm, but remember - *'practice makes perfect.'*

PSYCHIC TECHNIQUES

Inner space, the last frontier: to go where few have gone before.

Don't we just love to hear those fascinating stories of dreams coming true, seeing ghosts and having mystical experiences in some wonderful spiritual realm? Experienced meditators will tell you that to achieve such heights requires many years of practice. In the past and perhaps even today monks bricked themselves into caves for years with their only contact being a bowl of water and some food delivered by their student. To achieve spiritual bliss do we really need to go to such extreme lengths?

The practice of meditation can and does produce the most remarkable mystical experiences. I have found that sometimes one session of hypnotherapy is often enough to produce those same results. Some people reported that they felt so relaxed that they found themselves floating out of the chair and above their body during the session. These reports demonstrate that the trance state produced by hypnosis is much the same as experienced by meditators. It may take only one session to achieve what dedicated meditators strive for over a lifetime.

The practice of self hypnosis can put you into states that enable your psyche to develop. I recommend that you first visit a hypnotherapist for a few sessions to learn what it feels is like to be in trance. Once you know what it is like it is much easier to reproduce on your own.

To perform these exercises I suggest you become familiar with the trance state first. Without the ability to go into a very deeply relaxed state most of this section will just seem like fantasy.

Astral travel - Lucid dreaming - Dream body

Astral travel - The astral plane is the place where we sometimes do our dreaming. It is solid and magical. We have the ability to manipulate and change our astral environment. When we are flying we are in the 'astral' plane and 'astral traveling'.

Lucid dreaming - This is a visual experience in which we become aware that we are dreaming and can observe it unfold. When we enter the dream it then becomes astral travel.

Dream body - Also called the 'energy body' which we use in out-of-body experiences. It is not solid except when in the astral plane.

Through the diligent practice of the techniques outlined in this book you may eventually be able to have these same experiences.

The technique of entering the astral plane requires a very deep trance state. In fact so deep that you may often wake and forget the experience. Or you fall asleep before you wake up. It is not easy and most people, even experienced meditators, often fall asleep and forget their magical experiences.

Energy centres and kundalini (life-force)

We are beings made up of many vortexes of spinning energy which is also called life-force, chi, prana and kundalini. This passes through and connects our physical and spiritual bodies. The chakras (Indian Sanskrit for centres or vortexes) are generally associated with the endocrine glands and nerve plexus (large junctions of nerves), creating powerful energy fields.

These chakras command huge amounts of our energy. By expanding these energy fields we can access incredible levels of awareness not normally available. It is important to note that these chakras are powerful doorways to the astral planes and psychic phenomenon.

Dreaming and astral travel

One method of entering the astral planes is to wake up inside your dreams. Before you go to sleep create an environment like a sanctuary of where you would like to go. Use your goal setting and create a 1st person perspective of it. Make your kinesthetic body very excited, feel the excitement of astral travelling, feel your body tingling at the thought of entering this state. Drift off to sleep with this expectation.

Another technique is to *catch* yourself dreaming. I first found myself in the astral planes by waking up in my dreams. The feeling is fantastic, almost indescribable as you find yourself buzzing with energy. This buzz is your life-force surging through you, this is the 'kundalini experience' that you read about. You can develop this energy through these exercises, and with enough energy you can have these same experiences. The more life-force or energy you have the greater your chances to lift off.

Each night before you go to sleep and in your self hypnosis sessions, program your dreams using the goal setting and 1st person perspective. Aim to wake up while dreaming - inside your dream. Practice this each evening as you fall asleep.

Third eye - 'seeing' and astral travel

Some people use the 3rd eye to enter the astral plane. Focus your awareness on the area between your eyes in the middle of your forehead. This feels warm and can tingle or even expand as you power-up your 3rd eye for 'seeing'. As you enter the trance state you will feel almost a falling sensation - a dizziness as you drop deeply into trance. From here keep expanding your 3rd eye until you begin to visualise whatever you programmed yourself to see or experience.

Distant or Remote Viewing

This involves seeing objects, people or events while in a light trance state. It is like looking through a telescope. You will need to fixate on the desired vision and with practice you can see remotely in time and space. You can use the same method outlined in the *'third eye'* section.

I have worked with clients who have used this to view the planets and even to check out what was going on at home while they were in trance. A friend used it to find a special tool that went missing from his workshop. A client once went forward in time to discover a healthy and clean planet free of pollution and hatred. Use your discretion as to what you distant view and please don't invade someone's privacy without their explicit permission.

Wayne once went into trance and directed his awareness into a small, wire framed pyramid. Inside that pyramid (and unknown to Wayne) was a small bottle of scented oil. He came out of trance complaining that the pyramid was overpowered by the smell of sandalwood. There was no way he could have know this.

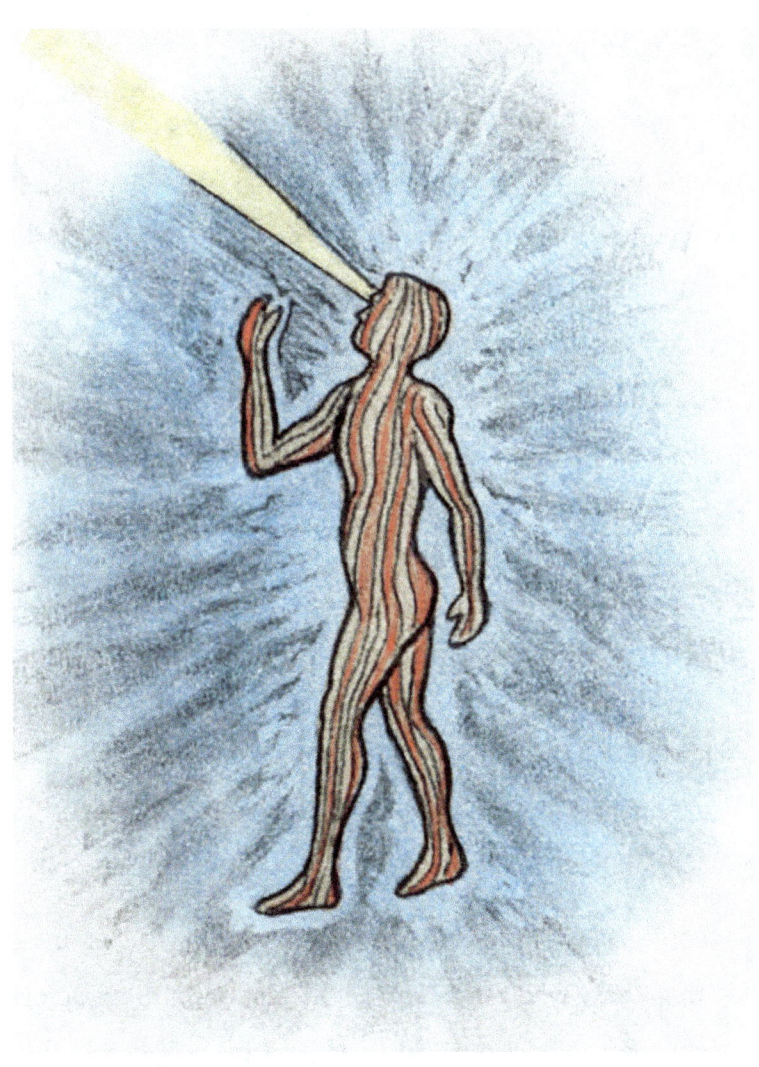

It is not necessary to go deeply into trance to do this particular exercise. Imagine that you are there, involve all your senses much like the third eye and distant viewing exercises.

Guided imagery, fantasy and the inner guide

Guided imagery is always an enjoyable way to move out of our ordinary existence and into the dream states. Create the image of your destination using your goal setting exercise. As you enter the trance state imagine yourself there. If you wish you can imagine an inner guide that represents the wisdom aspect of your subconscious on a more visible level. Perhaps an archetype such as the Sun or Moon, alchemist or wizard, a wicca or witch, Merlin the Magician, The High Priestess of tarot or the Greek Goddess Demeter. Who you choose as your inner guide is only limited by your imagination.

The secret to success is to be so determined that you don't give up. Create your goal, use your techniques and stick with it. By now you should have found the self hypnosis techniques that work best for you. Use them diligently until you have achieved some of the experiences outlined in this book.

Some people can visualise very easily. They can sometimes succeed quicker than those who need to go very deeply into trance before they visualise anything. However, strongly visual people can sometimes find that they can't relax deeply enough to enter those astral planes. Find your strongest modality (visual, auditory or kinaesthetic) and stick with it until you can start to access the other modalities.

Out-of-body experience (OOB)

Some people experience leaving their body during trauma such as in an accident, during an operation, witnessing something frightening or when they die and come back to tell about their experience. They are able to witness events but are unable to influence them.

In this experience you are able to walk through walls and move instantly to places around the world or beyond. To initiate out-of-body experiences you need to put in a lot of practice to achieve a deep trance state.

As you feel yourself getting lighter and lighter allow your dream body to sit up, roll over or stand while you visualise the room from each perspective. This is very much a 1st person perspective meditation.

There are two aspects to work on:

(1) *Perspective* - practice visualising from various positions around the room, from the ceiling or in the doorway. Then imagine looking through your own eyes from a sitting position or floating above your body.

(2) *The kinaesthetic body* - to experience standing or sitting by shifting your kinaesthetic (feeling) body to a place where you physically aren't. Practice with your favourite technique and feel yourself float out of your body while imagining yourself from that perspective. Sometimes imagining that you are wriggling and shifting

inside your body works. This means that you feel yourself in your body at various localities. Start by imagining it.

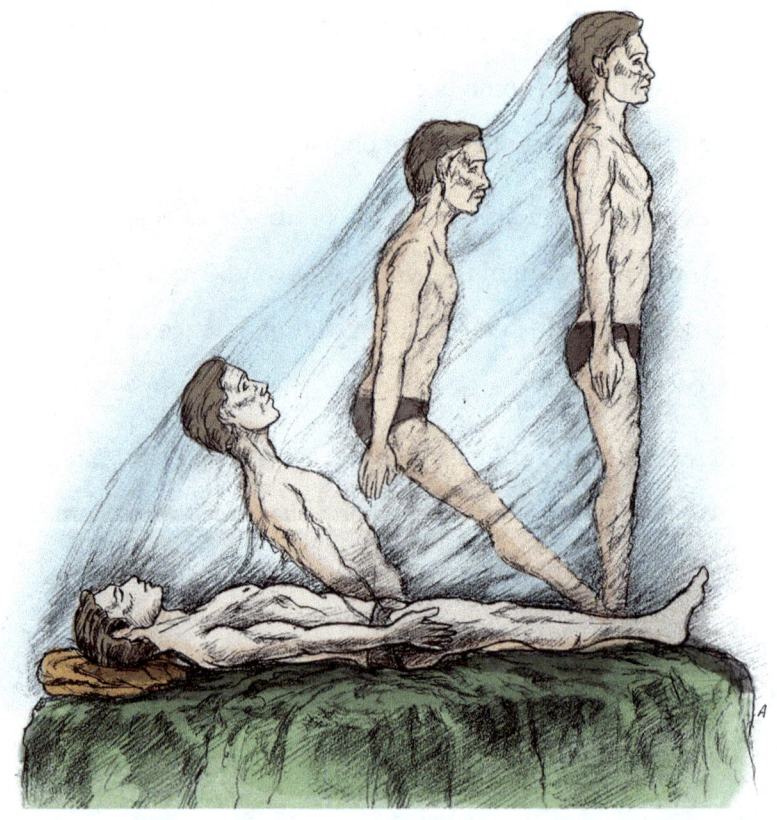

Some books suggest that you practice looking in the mirror to see yourself from various angles - try that too. Out-of-body experiences are part of the trance experience but needs a lot of practice.

Astral travel vs out-of-body experiences

I've had many adventures on the astral plane so much so that I became bored with them. I wanted to leave my body and walk through walls and visit people I knew. My aim was to have more out-of-body (OOB) experiences. But each time I came out of my body I found myself on some astral plane, a dream plane, instead of the here and now.

The astral plane is as real as this one which we live in every day. Things are solid to the touch and you can't walk through the walls. There is a degree of magic on this plane too and you can, with practice, create to your heart's content. The out-of-body experience (OOB) is where you leave your body and stay on the Earth plane. In that state you can walk through walls and are essentially like a ghost.

This particular night I awoke inside a dream and found myself in the astral plane. But I was convinced I was out-of-body at last. I walked towards the door so that I could visit some friends sleeping in their beds. I wanted to see if I could contact them. As I walked towards the door I decided to take a short cut through the wall, just to feel what it was like to walk through a wall. So I turned towards the wall and kept walking - but the wall was rock solid. I woke up with a sore face and my nose throbbed all night. That is an experience that I will never forget.

Protection

If you are worried about finding negative entities while you are out in the astral planes you can try this:

• Make your goal setting very strong in the 1st person.

• Include a sanctuary that is safe and secure.

• Do your astral traveling there in your sanctuary.

• Use a guide to escort and protect you.

• Develop your trance skills to the point that you can go in and out of trance easily.

• Remind yourself that if anything scary happens, you will always just wake up.

The fact is most astral travel is solitary and you will rarely find others on the same plane as yourself. Use the Alpha Omega technique more than any of the others because it provides an extremely safe environment from which you can explore the astral realms.

Flying

Flying is quite common and an exhilarating experience. To initiate flying in the trance state find yourself in your dream then jump upwards. Sometimes you can climb a small hill or a car top and leap into the air and fly. Always do a reality check before jumping off anything dangerous though. Usually this is not a problem because you will know that you are dreaming or in the astral plane. Another safer technique is to run and then leap into the air and start flying. That is a technique I have known others to use. Give it a go yourself.

Opening the Chakras - Energy Centres

My personal experience of opening chakras while practicing tai chi and Taoist meditations. For instance it took me eight years to open my heart chakra. I felt a surge of energy through my whole body like an electric shock and shook for several minutes. It finished with the most wonderful sense of joyfulness.

When I open my heart chakra now I basically open all my energy chakras. It happens automatically. My body wisdom knows to open everything at once. When I open my heart chakra my whole body will awake and chi will stream through my body. I then relax to allow it to flow, it feels like heaven.

When I began opening my chakras as a novice I would get headaches and heart palpitations. When I began to open my crown chakra I would get dizzy and become semiconscious. I then decided to do it at night in bed only, which I found was the safest way to do it.

When my crown chakra did open I had the most amazing experiences on the astral plane. They would sometimes last all night but the next two days I would be spaced out and suffer a mild headache. I always need to make sure I do my Earthing and practice Taoist Water meditations to manage these powerful forms of meditation.

Kundalini

I have tried to use the words most suitable to describe what adepts feel in reality. Kundalini is an Indian Sanskrit word that means large amounts of energy or life force (prana, chi). 'Kundalini awakening' is a term that is used to describe a rush or surge of energy. Generally from the Base Chakra. We can replace the word Kundalini with life-force. Once we awaken our kundalini we can awaken it in any chakra, organ or body part and even outside our body. If we awaken it in our Heart Chakra it is still a kundalini awakening. We can awaken our kundalini anywhere and it will still feel like an explosion of energy.

Kundalini and Astral Travel

What does kundalini feel like for me? It is like electricity shooting from my feet all the way through my body and out through the top of my head. It can happen automatically when asleep and it can trigger astral traveling. I often come back to really itchy thighs and legs because the energy is still roaring through me. It is very much a genuine physical phenomenon.

I once had a dream that I was driving along a bush track and accidentally drove over a cliff. Things then all went black, pitch black and I could feel a falling sensation. It seemed to go on forever and I realised that I would die. When that thought entered my head I stopped being afraid. It felt strangely nice, even though I was falling to my death.

As I fell I started to feel strange as though I was about to leave my body. Just then some dogs began fighting outside and the noise woke me up. I woke up right in the middle of leaving my body. I was able to analyse the process of initiating an astral experience.

I could feel energy strongly entering my feet, surging up my legs and into my torso. It was not restricted to just my spinal cord either. Then it was like a fire hose roaring out of the top of my head. I was buzzing and physically vibrating. The energy was roaring through me like a freight train. Once again I felt itchy all over my legs and thighs when I came back to my body - that is always very annoying.

As I lay there in bed I mused at how fascinating this process was. I had never been awake when I left my body like this before. Not right in the middle of it. Nearly all of my OOB and astral travel experiences have been after I had fallen asleep or in deep meditation. I rarely leave my body unless I am so deep I am unaware of the actual moment of leaving.

Ghosts

I have met quite a few ghosts on the other side while OOB. Many times it has been family members, close friends and sometimes with their own guides and advisers. I even had an interesting experience with a peeping-tom on the other side. Let me tell you about it.

My wife and I were staying at the in-laws and were both sound asleep. In the middle of the night I felt something not right and spontaneously OOB in the bedroom. I saw a man standing in our room watching us sleeping. I got the distinct feeling that he was not a nice person. Instinctively I yelled at him. He looked at me in absolute terror. I suspect that no one had ever confronted him like this before. He bolted through the wall in fright.

My meditation group was once asked to visit a friend's house which appeared to be haunted. Things moved, changed places, lots of spooky things were happening. We sat at the dinner table and meditated. One of our group, my good friend Al, said that it was a lost soul, an old man who had died some years ago.

That night I found myself OOB soon after I went to bed and floated over to this house. Sure enough there he was, a nasty old man. He had whiskers and a beard just like the gold digger character, Stinky Pete, from "Toy Story". He really was a mischievous old man.

I intuited that he got his kicks from scaring people. The same thing happened as before with the peeping-tom. I got boiling angry at him and told him to leave and stop misbehaving, to go to the light. I actually went up to him and kicked him in the pants. He went flying over the fence. His little legs were like windmills as he raced away into the distance.

When I came back to consciousness I was amazed at my reaction. Why did I get so angry with him? Why wasn't I nice and calm? Why didn't I guide him to the light? I have thought this through many times and the only conclusion I have was that my intuition took over from my rational mind. I am not normally an angry person. My intuition realised this ghost was not going to budge. He had survived many a ghost busting exercise in the past. My intuition knew that this fellow needed a swift kick up the pants to force him to move on and wake up to himself. I didn't think that he was stuck here but rather enjoyed annoying people on the Earth plane.

Haunted house

At another time I was asked to remove a ghost that was haunting an old farm house. I met the lady who was renting with her children and she pointed out the places where strange and frightening things had happened. I walked around the property to see the house from the outside and to get a feel for it. I then came home to meditate and see what was happening inside that closed room she was too terrified to open.

I easily entered trance and put my mind into the room that the woman said was haunted. I found that particular room and it was literally filled with spirits - and I mean filled to capacity. There were some really nasty ones too. I sensed a lot of evil. I felt there had been ritualised abuse, sexual abuse, alcohol and drug use. It was very unpleasant in there. I felt frightened for the first time in many years.

I wasn't there long before I was kicked out of the room. I was standing and viewing the partying adults, no longer living entities. They turned towards me. They knew I was there. I tried to stay but I lasted only about thirty seconds on each of the three occasions I made the attempt to contact them. They weren't going to leave.

After being kicked out on the last attempt I felt a sharp pinch on my little finger. I was sitting in meditation in my lounge chair at home when a little girl appeared right next to me and said, "Hi!" Then she pinched me, hard, she disappeared with a giggle.

I advised the lady who was living there of what I had experienced. The poor woman left with her children the following day. The entire family had been so traumatised by events in the house that they even left the entire region.

Astral black blobs

In my early days of astral travel I became aware of two black blobs of energy in the hallway outside my bedroom. I was in that twilight state halfway between awake and asleep. I realised that these two entities were searching for me. They had found my bright energy most attractive. I was a novice with loads of energy and they wanted some. Just as I realised what they were after my Tan Tien (navel chakra) went "crunch" inside me and I catapulted into another astral dimension. I literally disappeared.

Now this has happened only a few times when things had become unpleasant on the astral plane. It seems that my intuition takes control and I just disappear, to where I have no idea. I was somewhere safe. I don't know how long I was gone for.

When I came back to my body I again sensed the two black blobs. They were still out there in the hallway. They were silent and very still, uncertain of what to do next. It appeared that they had lost my scent. When I came back they must have sensed my energy because in desperation they raced towards me. I saw them lunge at me through the wall.

As soon as I sensed their desperate surge towards me my stomach went 'crunch' and I disappeared once more. This time I didn't come back for a very long time. When I eventually came back to my body they were gone and I went straight to sleep.

It happened again some time later. I was in a dream and I can't remember what was going on but all of a sudden I found myself awake – but not in this dimension. It was as though I was floating in outer space. I was no longer dreaming. Somehow I had slipped out of my dream and into one of the lower astral planes. I felt more than a little afraid this time. Just then I sensed some entities nearby and my stomach physically tightened into a knot of energy and I disappeared. These two experiences are about the only negative experiences I have ever had on the astral plane.

I met those two black blobs one more time. I now know what they do. This is from my dream diary - *I was practicing water meditation by breathing light into my body and surrounding myself with glowing golden light. It felt powerful yet subtle. I do it at night in bed and while sleeping. So far I have gone 'dreaming' two nights in a row. Last night was a full moon. I was breathing in the energy rays of the full moon. I must have fallen asleep because I dreamed that I had been shot in the head and chest. The shock forced me out of my body and I immediately astral travelled, flying around the dream-scape itself. It was so beautiful.*

I stopped flying and asked to be guided to perform some healing where it was needed. I found myself looking down on a man lying on the street. He was unconscious and being tended by another person leaning over him. I sensed that he was a drug addict. I then noticed my old friends those two black blobs of astral energy. They were patiently standing beside him waiting to drain him of some of his energy.

These black blobs don't appear to come from the earth plan. They exist in some other dimension. They are essentially harmless except that they like to feed upon human energy. They are energy suckers or something like that. Just imagine them as leaches. They won't kill you but they can be annoying. This drug addicted guy was wide open to them - his aura was wide open. I touched his third eye to close his aura which would stop those black blobs from stealing his energy.

Immediately I touched his third eye I came straight back to my body. I woke up with the most itchy legs.

My previous astral experience that night was via a vision. I was walking around a large farm yard looking for someone. But no-one was there. I then decided to go flying so I 'extended' my energy out of my feet and head and off I went flying. It was so wonderful. I flew higher and higher and I began to smile in great happiness. I was so happy and realised that this was the most wonderful experience I have ever had.

Kundalini man

While I am discussing kundalini this is another experience from my diary:- *I was doing some controlled dreaming one morning and found myself at a dam site beside a river. I saw an extremely tall man. He was three times as tall as an average person. He had a pointed short black beard which made him look something like the Jack of Spades from a deck of playing cards. I went over to him. I grew to his size and shook his hand. I asked him if he was a representation of something within me. He said, 'Yes'. I asked his name and he said very clearly, 'Kundalini'. I then asked if he had anything to say to me or to give me. He simply replied just as my dream experience began to fade, 'Use me more.'*

Once or twice I have found myself in the 'halls of wisdom'. A lovely university type place with massive wide lawns and garden and a lot of people. I wasn't able to stay very long though I was able to observe and admire the architecture and watch the people walking about. I was still a novice and maintaining focus for any length of time was difficult.

Some tips to help you

I try to avoid staring or becoming too involved with the visual aspects on my trips. If I stare too long at one object I generally come back to my body. If I keep active the experience will continue. This is also determined by the amount of energy at my disposal. If my energy is strong I can stay out on the astral plane longer.

In one astral experience I met one of my meditation teachers here on Earth. She was there with me on the astral plane. I felt myself coming back to my body so I asked her to give me some energy so that I could stay longer. She did as I requested by simply reaching out and touching me. I felt her powerful energy enter my dream body and I was able to stay with her for a much longer period of time. I have also done the same thing for others. I hold their hands to connect them with my energy while OOB or on the astral plane.

The very worst thing that can happen to you on the astral plane is that you fall asleep and forget everything that happened. You will not die or have a stroke. When you feel yourself falling in a dream it is exactly the same feeling that you get when OOB and astral travelling. It appears to be the beginning of your astral experience. Next time it happens go with it and see where it takes you.

If you are suddenly woken while OOB you will generally come back with a headache and feel really grouchy for some time. The best thing to do is have a shower or just sleep it off. The most common thing is to fall asleep towards the end of the experience but most of the time it is so exciting that you wake up and remember it quite well.

Write your experiences in a journal so that you have a record of your adventures. They are just too easy to forget otherwise.

The teachers that you find on the astral plane are usually genuine and they have your welfare at heart. But some are not so genuine depending on your amount of energy. So always do your preparation first. That way you will rarely, if ever, have any unpleasant experiences. I have never been attacked on the astral plane apart from the two experiences I have related to you. However I do know of people who do get attacked regularly. One suffers from schizophrenia and the others are either alcoholic or dabblers in spiritualism. Stay away from drugs because that is a stupid way to try and gain enlightenment – there are no short cuts.

Dreaming the future saved my family

I had a dream one Friday night. I was driving along a road that curved to the left slightly as it climbed a hill. As I was driving up this hill I was struck with a blinding light. It was like the sun was in my eyes. I couldn't see the road and something was about to happen. I didn't know what it was but it was not going to be nice. My inner voice said, *"It's inevitable, let's run through that again."*

The same scene was repeated: I couldn't see a thing from the blinding light then it finishes. The voice says, *"Yep, nothing can be done about it, it is inevitable."*

That Sunday around 1:00 pm we left to visit my parents several hours drive away and I had completely forgotten about the dream. At about 3 pm on a winding narrow road I was driving behind a car towing a large caravan. The caravan wheel kept hitting the dirt on the side of the road sending rocks and stones flying into my windscreen. The road began to climb up a hill when it divided into two lanes providing an opportunity for me to pass it.

I was becoming very frustrated with this idiot in front of me and so I pulled out and began to pass him. The sun was at such an angle that afternoon that I couldn't see the road ahead very clearly. The road then began to curve to the left which placed the sun right in my line of vision blinding me. Just as I was halfway past the caravan itself the driver began to move his vehicle across the road towards me.

I hadn't realised that the lane had ended and that the caravan was pulling back into the single lane. I was now on the wrong side of the road, but because the sun was in my eyes I didn't even know it.

I had nowhere to go. Just then my dream flashed into my mind and I immediately slammed on the brakes and pulled in behind the caravan - just as two cars sped past my window. It was a matter of a split second. *"Just like my dream."* I thought to myself. My wife turned to me and said, as she usually does when I am driving, *"You damned idiot."*

PAST LIFE THERAPY

Believing that you have lived before is not necessary for you to flashback to a past life experience. Wayne wanted to give up smoking and spontaneously experienced a past life. Over a number of sessions the story of a young man who had lived a short life in Wales early last century unfolded.

"Shhh. Be quiet, they're singing," Wayne said during his hypnotherapy session.

This young man had gone to the rescue of a family in a burning house while on his way home from working in the coal mines. He saved the family but was trapped. The last thing he remembers was breathing smoke which burned the back of his throat.

Wayne loved to smoke strong tobacco, so strong that it burnt the back of his throat. He was reliving his death experience as a smoker. That same year he was posted to England for training. He hired a car and drove to that same village in Wales. He found his gravestone in the cemetery.

There have been numerous experiences like Wayne's that have been authenticated by serious researchers. They may never be accepted by mainstream science but that is the nature of society today.

As a therapy re-experiencing your past lives can provide insight into the most pressing issues you are experiencing. However, not all current problems can be traced back to a past life. Most are created here in this one and are best dealt with by other means.

Past life therapy can also provide interesting insight into where you have been. Not all past lives were traumatic so don't expect a violent death or some other dramatic existence. Most people recall a rather mundane existence, usually with a current close family member. Sharing life as husband or wife are common. Often swapping roles lifetime after lifetime as partners, a child or parent, brother or sister. It seems that we incarnate together to work out our problems coming back time and again to try and get it right. They may not always incarnate as friends but meet up lifetime after lifetime to learn the lessons specific to each individual.

Past life murder

Lesarra had just broken up with her boyfriend of some years, she felt that something was just not right about their relationship. She went quickly into trance to find herself living in a cold, damp castle. Her current boyfriend was there, he was involved in a religious cult and this really frightened her. When she tried to stop him participating in their activities he turned on her in a fit of rage and stabbed her to death.

As sad as this appears Lesarra could now accept why she had left this fellow. Over the months that followed she changed. Normally a reserved, fearful young lady, Lesarra became more assertive and grew as an individual. This is one of the most common outcomes of this therapy: to change for the better through the insight gained doing past life regressions.

Feeling - emotional traces

Warning, this technique can make you very emotional and is best used under a therapist's supervision.

Use the self hypnosis technique that works best for you and enter a light trance state.

To trace your emotional problem back into the past:

(1) Feel your sadness, loneliness, anger or whatever emotion it is that is bothering you.

(2) Build upon the feeling until an image forms.

(3) Expand this image until you can follow what is happening around you.

(4) Observe the events as they unfold, use the 3rd and 1st person perspectives, knowing that you can change perspective at will and wake up at any time.

(5) When you awaken write down everything that happened. Review it over the next few days to note how it has affected your life now. The recording and debriefing stage is very important.

This technique is an emotional one, use with caution as you may become quite upset. I recommend that you talk to your therapist before you try this method. Better still, discuss how you can do this in therapy with them, perhaps using some of the other techniques first.

Mists of time - the bridge

Enter a deep trance, perhaps start with the Alpha Omega technique:

(1) Imagine that you are standing on a bridge.

(2) Halfway along the bridge there is a heavy mist. Using your 1st person perspective walk into the mist.

(3) Allow yourself to spin much like in a time tunnel until you find yourself either in an image of the past or on the other side of the bridge with the mist clearing.

(4) Observe what is happening around you, take note of the clothes and shoes that you are wearing.

(5) Move about and try to recognise the place, people or the feelings that it evokes - use your intuition to understand what this experience may be about.

This technique is best done in deep trance to by-pass the fantasy stage. To prove a past life experience beyond doubt will require many sessions with details on places, dates and names. If you wish to use this method why not try the services of a therapist to initiate your sessions.

Cycling through relationships

Janet experienced feelings of being trapped and panicked when confronted by stressful situations. In trance she found herself in the hull of a war galley rowing for her, no, his life. She saw that she was male and firmly chained to the inside of a wooden ship. During the naval battle her ship was rammed, Janet and her fellow rowers were trapped, they all drowned.

Janet had conflict with her husband, nothing serious but their constant clashes for control was enough to concern her. Through these sessions she discovered that they had been brothers in an Indian tribe and fought for control after their father had died. It was here that the competition between them began. This was replayed time and again through several more lifetimes as each strove to win over the other with wit and strength. Each life involved different family roles, one would be the mother, father, brother, sister, wife or husband to the other. With this insight Janet was able to work with her husband to recognise that their competitive behaviour was destroying their relationship.

One time in the Holy Land

I've used the bridge technique myself, I like its simplicity. In one such session I found myself in the Holy Land, Syria, during one of the many Christian Crusades. I was an attendant to a powerful yet stupid Knight. I could clearly see him sitting astride his horse in the middle of a large caravan of pack horses and camels. We were traveling slowly, weaving our caravan through the scrubby desert hills when we were attacked by bandits wielding swords and spears. They appeared to be experienced in killing. It all happened so fast. I was left standing beside my Knight's horse, without any weapons. I watched from a position above myself as a raggedly-dressed bandit rode past swinging his curved sword. His stroke almost separated my head from my body. I now know why I feel so uncomfortable when someone touches my throat.

Between Lives

To go into that space between lives is always fascinating. Regress yourself back to birth and then ease yourself between lives. For example, find yourself in a garden with your inner guide and ask what lessons you are to learn in your forthcoming life. What experiences will you be challenged to overcome? Ask whatever questions comes to mind. Sometimes you will get some strange answers as your fantasies get in the way of true insight. To work through fantasy perform this same exercise three times. The third time will usually provide the deepest insight.

Aheb found himself in a garden with a gentle old man. They were talking of his future life on Earth. He was crying. He did not want to reincarnate and relive the trauma that he had experienced in his previous few lives. By gaining insight into these lessons, to learn 'compassion and tolerance', he was able to see a clearer path for living. It allowed him to come to terms with his life. A little insight can certainly help in troubled times.

Time travel – the time tunnel

The only limitations in time and space are those you impose on yourself. If you wish to travel forward in time then you can just as you can travel backwards in time. However what you experience is from your own perspective and limited by your belief systems. But then again don't let that limit you.

Imagine that you are in a time tunnel. Allow it to spin you forward or backwards. Using your kinesthetic body, feel the spinning and allow yourself to become slightly disoriented. When this happens will yourself to travel forwards or backwards in time and to then become aware of where you end up. When the spinning stops, check your surroundings using your visual, auditory and kinesthetic senses. Try to gain some understanding of your destination and its environment.

Matt once used this technique to astral visit a prehistoric period and had a close encounter with a huge wild animal. He came off second best and could feel the claw marks on his body when he opened his eyes. I find that the 'distant viewing' and 'third eye' techniques are more useful and a lot safer when you travel to places or times you think may be dangerous.

The Battle for New Orleans - War of 1815

Dale came for hypnotherapy because he had a recurring dream of being killed in battle. He wanted to find out about the flashing lights that woke him in the middle of the night. In his session he was guided to separate from his body, to leave it and fly over the battlefield.

He saw several old sailing ships pulled onto the sands at the edge of a broad river. He saw reeds, swamps and trees, but no battlefield as we would expect in this day and age. As he dropped closer he saw piles of food, ammunition and other stores haphazardly thrown together as ant-like people carted objects off the ships and made ready in preparation for their invasion.

Soldiers in various battle dress milled about seemingly directionless and it appeared to be a complete shambles. Then, excitedly, he noticed his dream soldiers: *"There, down among the reeds, two soldiers in full tartan battle kit. I wonder what regiment they are? They are carrying heavy, long barreled rifles, they have bayonets on the ends. They're pushing through these high reeds. It's dusty, I can see they are sweating, it's really hot inside those woollen jackets. The poor beggars, they can't see a darn thing."*

These two scouts had been sent out to reconnoitre their position and find out where they had landed. At least someone knew what to do, he thought. Then he realised that he is, or was, the lead scout.

"This is my dream. I'm pushing through the reeds that are so thick you can't see more than a foot in front of your face. We were all so very afraid of the American snakes and spiders. The heat is stifling, the dust is choking and we are both quite exhausted."

He can remember how their movement stirred the dust from the dry reeds and how it drifted into their eyes and noses threatening to choke them.

He dropped downwards into his physical body to become one with the Scottish soldier. He was the more experienced of the two, a lead scout, pushing, heaving through the reeds with his heavy rifle and backpack. His bayonet kept getting in the way of their progress, annoying him. It is the American War of Independence and he is part of the British push to control those rebellious American settlers.

All of a sudden he broke free of the swampy reeds to stand on the edge of a dry creek bed. He stared at the large puddles of muddy water in front of him. He instinctively looked across the creek to the opposite bank. Over an expanse of only ten or so yards he saw a flash of many bright lights and then nothing. Both he and his loyal friend died that morning. They were killed by the very Americans he had so excitedly set forth from his home in the Scottish highlands to tame.

Dale then found himself floating above two graves marked by piles of rocks and wooden crosses. It was down an embankment in the dry creek bed itself, beside a young, crooked willow tree. He said out loud, *"They have the wrong names on them, they've got it 'arse-about'."*

I directed him back to the ships and the landing parties who slowly, like ants, were building stores of supplies ready for the invading troops. He slowly came back to consciousness, satisfied that he now had confirmation of his dream. It was the Battle of New Orleans, January 1815. He could now reconcile himself in that dramatic event of 200 years ago.

He soon stopped suffering those recurring nightmares from his time in the motorised cavalry. They disappeared after seeing those alluring flashes of light that had haunted his dreams. The lights were, of course, the flash from the many muzzles of enemy rifles from the other side of the creek. Now that he knew he could sleep in peace.

Some two years later Dale and his partner visited the memorial park near New Orleans where he died in that long-past incarnation. It was a hot day as he leaned against an ancient, crooked willow tree. It bent over the edge of a dry creek bed. The heat was suffocating and his mind was in a daze, he wasn't quite there. His partner then called out, *"Dale, look at those two graves, what do those signs say?"*

Dale told me that he nearly passed out, *"It hit me like a rock. I was leaning on the willow tree just like I had seen in my dreams. I was looking directly at the two graves in the dry creek bed, just like in my dream. I knew which grave was mine and that it had the wrong damn name on it. We both were so excited. I could finally give that brave young soldier my deepest gratitude. Now he could rest in peace."*

SPIRITUALISM AND CLAIRVOYANCE

A good way to develop your psychic ability is to believe in yourself and to then do it yourself. The best psychics are regular meditators and so have a good understanding of the workings of the unconscious. To assist you in developing your psychic abilities work steadily on your self hypnosis and focus on entering into the trance state easily. Once you can do this there are many paths for you to follow as discussed in this book.

Psychic readings - overheads, aura readings

When a psychic gives a reading without using aids such as, tarot cards, an astrology horoscope, psychometry; they call it an 'overhead' because they are looking 'over your head'. Overheads may also be called 'aura reading' as it involves much the same method. This is possibly the hardest of all psychic skills because the only anchor the psychic has is your physical presence. Many good psychics can use a photograph, hair or blood sample or name to locate and diagnose. I know a number of dowsers that diagnose their subject's health problems with only the person's name to guide them.

The late Muriel Morrison, one of South Australia's best known dowsers, came home one evening to find her house had been broken into. There was blood on the broken window where the burglar had entered. She took the blood sample and dowsed over a street map of the local area. The police were called and found her goods and the bandaged robber at the address she gave them.

One exercise you could try is to sit, close your eyes and visualise your client. As you do so use your body awareness to tune in and understand their physical illness or whatever it is they have asked your assistance with. Using this technique you will begin to experience sensations and insights regarding their health. You can go into the past, present or future at this point. I will repeat my earlier warning: make sure that you are grounded yourself before attempting this exercise. You wouldn't want to erroneously give them your own or someone else's health diagnosis.

The sandy beach

Wayne choked each time he relaxed to meditate, he could never go deeply into trance without waking suddenly in panic. I decided to help him uncover why this was happening. I put my hands on his back and neck as I tuned into him. Images and sensations began to form in my mind.

"I can see the beach, sand, there's sand… you want to yell for help, sand…" I kept coming back to to the word 'sand' and the need to scream for help. I could feel Wayne's panic. Just then Wayne jumped up from the chair and rushed to the bathroom to vomit.

"That's it!" he said afterwards. *"When I was 10 years old we were at the beach and I was playing with a boy I had just met. He was much

bigger than I was. He was very rough and sat on top of me and started to hit me. To stop me crying for help he shoveled sand into my mouth. I woke up in the hospital." Wayne had forgotten this incident completely and was surprised that he could forget such a traumatic event. After gaining this insight he no longer panicked when relaxing or meditating.

Dowsing - psychometry

Psychometry is a technique in which you gain insight into an object or a person by touch. Many psychics will use a watch or jewelry to connect and 'tune in' to their client. Some dowsers use the third eye technique. Others 'feel' into the object and 'sense' the owner's problems, future direction or the answers to questions they may have.

Frank Moody, at over 95 years of age was one of the best dowsers I have known. While he was staying with me, I spoke to a woman whose son was badly injured when his tractor rolled-over and crushed him. Frank was in NSW and her son was in far north Queensland some 2000 kilometres away. She told me that Frank had worked on her son by distant healing and had helped considerably with his brain damage and paralysis. Frank would place magnets on a map of this young man's brain from 2000 kilometres away. She was full of praise for his skill and ability.

Another time Frank was asked by a surgeon to find a blood clot in one of his patients. Frank dowsed its position and notified the doctor who was amazed when his tests found it exactly where he had indicated. To go one step further Frank broadcast healing to the patient and dissolved the clot which no longer required surgery.

As a hands-on healer Frank is at his best. My wife loves exercise but would become exhausted and her face was always bright red after each training session. Frank sensed from the other side of the room that her tricuspid valve was under-functioning. He then pointed his hands towards her chest to direct healing energy at the valve. My wife has not experienced exhaustion like that since nor does she look like a cooked lobster after exercise.

To learn dowsing it is best to contact your local dowsing society or find a local dowser to watch and learn from. There are many books on the subject and you can go to your library and start there. Better yet visit my good friend and master dowser Harald Tietze's web site at: http://www.wise-mens-web.com

Harald Tietze took a group of friends, including myself, to outback Lake Mungo, way out in the Australian desert. One member of the group wandered off and disappeared. We had no idea where she went. It's so easy to get lost in the vast expanse of the desert. Everyone was worried that we might not find her or that she had been injured and couldn't make her way back to us.

I watched as Harald went outside quietly by himself. He just stood there for a while. It was as though he was feeling the desert around him. He then jumped in his vehicle and drove to the exact spot where she was sitting some 5 kilometres away.

Automatic writing

There are many books in the new age stores that have been written by this method. They are said to be 'channeled' by higher sources.

Be warned though that not all channeled writings are from a higher source - it must first be filtered through the unconscious and therefore influenced by the individual's drives, urges and instincts. Note that your own automatic writing also comes from that same source, your unconscious. Is it really an entity you are channeling, your higher consciousness or is it your deeper unconscious?

One simple exercise in using automatic writing is for your own personal insight. Try writing immediately after you have come out of a self hypnosis session. Just as you waken reach for your pen and write whatever is in your head. Just allow the ideas and thoughts to flow. You will be surprised at what comes out using this method.

It sounds strange and quite frightening to think that you can write without consciously controlling the process or content but it is quite normal. We spend so much time in the unconscious that we take it for granted. For instance the act of driving your car or hitting a tennis ball is a complex process yet we can do it without thinking.

EEG BIOFEEDBACK - NEUROFEEDBACK

EEG Biofeedback is also called Neurofeedback or simply 'brain training'. This is a professional level, advanced technology that reads your brainwaves, EEG, then feeds this information back to the brain to improve its performance. This is done via playing a game or watching a movie where the screen will slightly change in contrast and volume in relation to what the brain is doing.

In my practice I did an enormous amount of biofeedback and brain training for such problems as disturbed sleep, anxiety, panic attacks, depression and peak performance. Unfortunately this is not a technology that you can just buy and use straight out of the box. It needs professional supervision and support to set your system up. You will need to know exactly what brainwave frequencies to train, how to use the software and where to place the leads for your individual symptoms or needs. Do not try this by yourself though, it really is a specialised field and you will need to see a professional, usually a psychologist, if you are interested.

Stories on the power of Neurofeedback

Eric arrived at my practice one morning in the arms of his loving mother who looked absolutely exhausted. Eric, an autistic two year old, was becoming just too much for this petite, single working mum. He looked around my office, smiled and then turned his head away, disconnecting himself away from our world and back into his own.

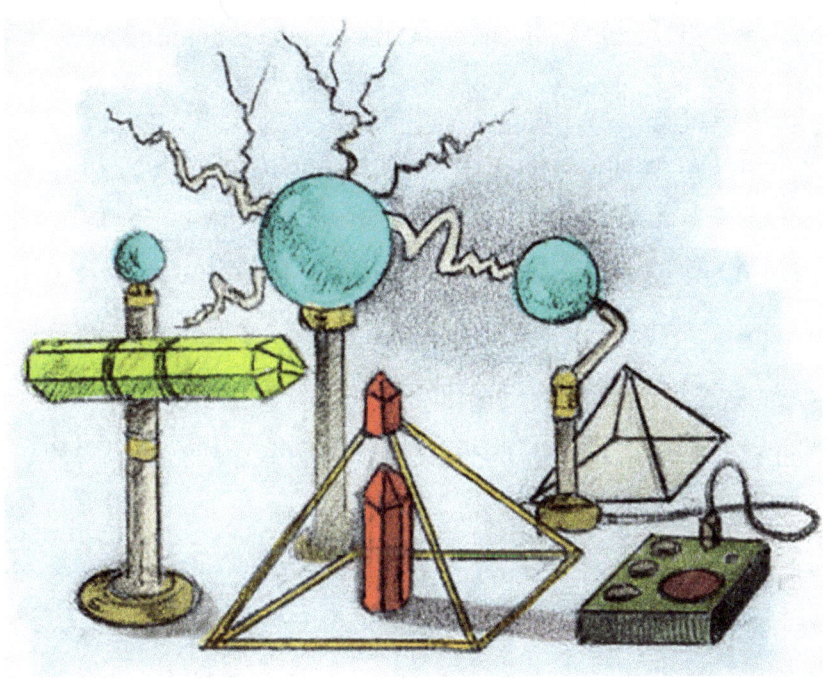

Mum explained that Eric wasn't sleeping. He kept waking every hour and throwing tantrums for what seemed to last all day long. He wouldn't take his bath, have a meal or go to bed without throwing a tantrum. He cried all the time and she was at her wits end ready to have a melt down herself.

I sat with Eric's mother and we chatted about what her options were. Raising an autistic child was hard work and simply too much for any single parent, especially one working full time to pay the bills. I asked her a lot of questions because I needed to know exactly what symptoms Eric was experiencing. I also needed to discover which brain hemisphere was his dominant hemisphere. It turned out that

Eric was right handed, which meant his dominant hemisphere was on the left, like all right-handers.

Generally we used neurofeedback with people sitting in a comfortable chair while they watch a movie which changes in contrast and volume - this is how we train their brainwaves. Eric didn't watch TV. I am not sure if he knew that TV even existed because he just turned away when we tried to introduce it to him. We needed some sort of feedback for his brain so that it could then train itself.

His mother told us that she played music at home and I found that we had the same music on our computers. While Michael Jackson played in the background Eric crawled along the floor opening my cupboards and drawers. He was wearing a wireless EEG biofeedback system clipped to his shirt which he completely ignored.

When Eric's brain was training in the direction it needed to go, the music would play uninterrupted. When his brainwaves went back to their dysregulated state the music would stop.

The sites I decided to train were the Central Sensory Motor Strip on the left hemisphere to improve his low muscle tone which would help him walk by himself. I also placed two leads on his right hemisphere: one on his right Temporal Lobe and another on his right Orbitofrontal Cortex, just above his right eye. These two placements would help him regulate his mood and behaviour. This was basically for his tantrums and to improve his sleep.

He initially trained every second day for two weeks by which time he was sleeping through the night and his tantrums had improved considerably. Within 4 weeks he walked in by himself much to his exhausted mother's joy. By week six he was sitting in his mother's lap watching the Wiggles on our monitor. He was laughing and clapping with them.

Within six weeks Eric was in the world we all share, no longer trapped in his own world. His mother was now smiling and radiant, a very happy mother. She was not only getting quality sleep but now saw a fulfilling life for herself and her son, where previously there was only hardship and sadness. She bought a home system and began training Eric herself.

This is just one simple story of the incredible power and potential of biofeedback, specifically neurofeedback. Let me tell you of a few more before I finish this book.

Jackson was injured in a motor vehicle accident experiencing a life-threatening brain injury. In the emergency room the surgeons wanted to turn off his life support. Jackson's parents successfully fought this in court to save their son's life.

When he was brought to my clinic for neurofeedback I saw this six foot four inch young man stretched out in a giant sized wheel chair. He was partially paralysed and his mind was elsewhere. He suffered seizures and his brain injury included his brain stem which connects the brain with the rest of the body. An injury like this is sometimes called "Locked-in Syndrome". Jackson may be fully aware of his environment yet completely unable to communicate. This happens when the nerves from the mid brain have been damaged by physical trauma.

It was heart wrenching to see and I thought to myself that I might not be able to fulfill the expectations of his loving family. Although with each session we weren't sure if he could see or hear we continued with his neurofeedback. His reward was an audible click each time his brain was training in a positive direction. A simple reward yet extremely powerful as you will soon see.

It was heart breaking to see him like this twice a week when he came with his family for training. But sure enough within two weeks his mother reported that he was more attentive. Even more exciting was that his sleep was starting to regulate. Eight years later he is speaking, singing, moving and engaging with his family and carers. Most importantly he can eat without a feeding tube in his stomach and he certainly enjoys his meat pies.

One of my greatest rewards was when Jackson's mother took me aside and said, *"Thank you for giving my son back to me."*

There is rarely anything more satisfying for a therapist than having someone tell you how much they look forward to seeing you. One client recently said, *"I couldn't wait to get back here after yesterday's training. For the first time in my life I woke this morning without thinking how much I wanted to die. Thank you."*

THE INNER DRAGON - MY JOURNEY BEGINS

My life is in chaos. I try to focus once again and breathe deeply, slowly. The feelings of exhaustion and stress cease to overwhelm me and I deliberately begin to sink into my inner world, into that place I call 'Pluto's Cave'.

I breathe out again and sink deeper, deeper still, my body dissolves. I break free of the outer world and I can see in the distance a mountain range. Through the haze and mist I head towards it in my astral body.

I release even more tension as I breathe out once again. I feel my astral body start to glow as more energy and power surges through me. I am flying over a dusty, barren plane of red sand heading towards the mountain range. I can feel the dry heat rising up to caress me from the desert flats below.

Beneath me winds a sluggish, muddy river cutting through the desert. On one side of the river is a tall, rocky mountain peak. On the other is a mountain range that ends in a cliff falling to the river below. I intuitively know that somewhere near the top of this range is a place of power. It is Pluto's Cave the entrance to my psyche, my inner world.

I feel the urge to go to this cave first. I pass over and around the mountain peak. It is sharp and rocky, nothing lives there it is totally barren. This is Capricorn, my astrological Ascendant sign that plays a powerful role in my life. Capricorn stands alone towering above the choking sands, jagged rocks and energy-sapping heat of the desert below.

From high in the air I spy Pluto's Cave. Lush, green ferns and long grass partly covers its entrance. I land among the ferns that contrast abruptly with the reddish desert sands. I can smell the eucalyptus oils in the warm air and hear the moaning wind as it rises from the desert below.

Just below my Capricorn Ascendant is the asteroid Chiron, known as the 'Wounded Healer' in Greek mythology. The Centaur, Chiron, was the wise teacher of heroes and heroines. He was an immortal like the Gods. As I stand at the entrance to Pluto's Cave, the portal to my deep Unconscious, the Underworld of Greek mythology, I look around its ferny entrance. I cannot see Chiron, he should be waiting to greet me.

Peering inside the cave I can faintly see someone squatting on the dirt floor. He appears prehistoric, a stone-age man. An animal hide covers his nakedness and he is hairy and unkempt. I'm so disappointed.

I can see a roughly built earthen fire sitting in the middle of the cave. A tumble of burnt sticks and old blackened ashes are scattered about the filthy cave floor. Chiron, appearing as a caveman, is sitting beside the fire. He looks towards me as smoke from his fire rises lazily into his face. He coughs as he wipes at his watering, bloodshot eyes. Does he even see me? Am I a ghost in his world? Is he really a part of me? Am I really that spiritually uncivilised?

With some trepidation I step into the cave. I stand awkwardly looking, waiting. With a lazy hand-gesture he invites me to sit beside him at his fire.

I think to myself, '*Maybe this is the Chiron archetype from a millennia ago. I guess I can accept him as Chiron, the Wounded Healer of Greek mythology, but this guy certainly is no King of the Centaurs.*'

I visit Chiron each day in my meditations. I find myself above the desert flats rising higher and higher into the air like an eagle and fly to Pluto's Cave. Each time I visit I try to understand what it is within me that has created him in this prehistoric form. Then on one visit a flash of insight hit me. I realised that I needed to empower him to raise his spiritual awareness. I needed him as an ally to help me on my inner journey.

Gesturing towards the cave entrance I led Chiron outside into the sunshine away from the gloom of the cave. There among the ferns I began to do tai chi. Moving slowly I would glance at him and nod "yes" when he copied me. I made sure that when I could feel the energy flow through my hands and navel centre (dan tien) that he could too. I entered his body with my mind to allow him to feel the flow of energy, to feel its power. He learned very quickly. I taught him to flow fire chi through his body.

One day I arrived to notice that he was dressed in rich flowing Chinese robes. He spoke to me not quite fluent English but he did speak. Chiron's cave was a place where I found solitude and peace from the crazy world outside. He had become my ally, my guide, Chiron the Wise. We would meditate together around his fire or do tai chi outside in the grass and among the green ferns. Here was my sanctuary and my ally and together we shared a stillness within.

On this day he told me that it was time to go beyond the reflections of the firelight on the cave walls. I had never thought to explore the darkness beyond. *"There be dragons,"* he whispered.

For some years I had been assisting my clients to rescue their own lost and wounded selves. Dragons had recently become a feature of my therapy and I wanted to explore this avenue personally. Now that I was pushed I decided to use this therapy myself.

I walked purposefully to the end of the cave. It opened up showing a dim light over a set of stairs that led into a gigantic cavern. Following the stone stairs downwards I saw my inner dragon. He had brilliant golden scales and fire flickered around his feet.

"I need to tame you because you're causing havoc in my life," I bravely called into the stillness of this foreboding cavern. The dragon fixed his gaze on me. He turned away from my voice and lazily, teasingly, rolled onto his back. I could see splashes of molten lava shoot up into the air around him. I wondered to myself, *'what is his name?'*

It was the end of my meditation. As I returned to consciousness I heard his voice inside my head: *'Freedom, my name is Freedom.'*

I meditated each day in Pluto's Cave with Chiron. We practiced tai chi among the ferns and sometimes I would go into a deeper meditative state while Chiron sent healing light into my body. I practiced these magical exercises but I just couldn't find a way to tame that wild dragon within me. Each night I would leave my body to travel to distant stars or I would speak to the wise ones on other dimensions - but no flash of insight came to show me how to tame my inner dragon. Then one night I had the dream I so desperately needed.

I was dreaming and woke to find myself inside the dream. I was walking along a dark and lonely street well after midnight. I realised that I was in the city slums. All was quiet and I was a little anxious. I heard a voice in my head say, *'This place is menacing.'*

I then noticed a teenager sitting alone on the street curb with his head in his hands. He was wearing a hoody pulled down to hide his face.

I walked closer and stopped to look at him. In shock I discovered that it was me. *'Oh my goodness that is me when I was a teenager.'* He looked up at me with a solemn face.

"What can I do to help?" I asked him. I knew that if this is what is inside my unconscious I needed to act.

He gave me a task to complete. It was so simple that I would never have guessed it in a million years. He then dropped his head in defeat as if he believed I would fail him.

Over the next few months I begin to change. I worked hard at enjoying life, I tried hard to focus on my family and friends rather than lock myself away to study. Using self hypnosis I went back into my past to find my lost inner selves to rescue them.

In my psychotherapy practice I guided wounded souls using this approach every day. I knew exactly what to do. I knew how to apply this same process to heal my own wounds. I knew that I had to do for me what I did for others: *"Healer, heal thyself."*

My own inner world had been barren, desolate and stressed. Only a small corner was flourishing: at Chiron's fireplace inside Pluto's Cave. One small corner of stability, a sanctuary in a parched landscape. That changed, not immediately but change it did.

Over an intense period of daily meditation and dreaming I sought to fully understand the process I had just completed. I discovered that my sad and fearful inner selves were feeding my dragon. His food was their fear, betrayal, confusion, mistrust, stress, abandonment and sadness. This was keeping my inner dragon restless, agitated and untameable.

By going within to find and rescue my inner selves from trauma I slowly eliminated my dragon's diet of negative emotions. He starved to death and was reborn within me as insight and awareness.

I know that I still have dragons in my underworld, but they are small and easily tamed. Freedom was the one I needed to tame first. These others want to be tamed they have no interest in challenging me they want to fly with me.

Wishing you every success in your practice to rescue your inner selves and tame your inner dragons. If you enjoyed this book please leave a review.

Regards

Noel Eastwood

December 2016

APPENDIX 1

Exploring the myths of hypnosis and clinical hypnotherapy

Of all the psychological therapies at our disposal, hypnotherapy and self hypnosis must be the most misunderstood. This is an explanation of many of the myths hypnotherapists encounter.

Just like everyone else I once believed the myths perpetuated on television and in the press. By looking into a hypnotist's eyes, I could fall into a trance and be compelled to do things against my will. I could fall into a hypnotic trance and as portrayed in one of Alfred Hitchcock's short stories - if the hypnotist fell down dead I would never wake up again. Scary thoughts indeed.

I personally found out how wonderful this therapy was when I was struggling with exam nerves at university. I sought treatment from a clinical hypnotherapist and that was the beginning of my incredible journey.

Myths:

Everyone will fall into trance immediately and do as the hypnotist says without exception

(1) Everyone is susceptible to hypnosis: Yes and no. Experience and studies have shown only about 70% of all people will fall into a light trance under a trained hypnotherapist. The other 30% will require many more sessions of training before they will be able to enter a

desirable level of trance. Some people will never allow themselves to relax enough to go into a trance state.

(2) Everyone is compelled to do exactly as the hypnotherapist says: Definitely no. Regardless of level of trance you will still maintain a strong level of awareness and balk at any command or suggestion that goes against your morals or induces fear. At times, going into a memory that is frightening will cause you to awaken and refuse to go further. Any immoral suggestion will cause the same reaction, even if in a very deep trance. Our critical faculty is ever present, even in the deepest trance.

What is more frightening is that suggestions to perform an act that may be against your better judgment is happening right now in the security of your living room. Just take a few moments next time you watch a commercial on television. Now ask yourself if what you see, hear and feel is inducing or suggesting you to do something against your better judgment. Ask yourself what methods are used by advertisers to convey their message. Do they use suggestion? Perhaps subliminal and not strikingly visible at first glance. Most people are in a very light trance when they watch TV and this is easily exploited.

I will go into trance in the first session

Wrong, most people require a few sessions to relax deeply in the presence of a stranger. The skills of the therapist may speed this process but it is usually once the first session is over that deep and useful states can be experienced. In the first session, you the client are discovering what trance feels like.

The therapist is also determining which technique is the best for you. At the end of the first session the therapist will encourage you to talk about what happened, which sense worked best (visual images, sounds and words, feelings, sensations, etc.), which part of the induction was the easiest, how did it feel. She then determines the best method to use next time and how to approach your induction in the future. Most people require 3 - 4 sessions before they are comfortable enough to enter trance easily. The important thing to remember is that we are all individuals and we all require an individual approach.

My friend was hypnotised and gave up smoking / weight loss / exam nerves / learned self hypnosis in just one session

Did they really or were they just saying that to impress you? Few people achieve lasting success from just one session. Many respected and experienced hypnotherapists refuse to see anyone unless they agree to attend a minimum of 6 sessions. Some therapists prefer to do the job properly and see their clients for at least 20 sessions.

Looking into the hypnotist's eyes will put me into a trance and under his will

Few hypnotherapists have the skill to use their eyes to put someone into trance. The great Milton Erikson was said to be one who could use his eyes, voice or a touch to put someone into trace as they sat and chatted – but that was only someone he had already been working with. As for being under their spell or command, you must first agree and allow them to do this. Apart from these examples the answer is 'no'.

The hypnotist will brain-wash me

Our unconscious critical faculty protects us. If someone was afraid of this happening then I am sure that they would not bother going to a hypnotherapist in the first place. Some religions perpetuate this common Hollywood-style myth for their own motives, which may be another form of immoral suggestion.

But what about stage hypnotists

There are many myths to be dispelled here:

(1) The hypnotist is very skilled and charismatic. They know the type of person who will come up on stage: *the idiot* who wants to disprove the hypnotist - she soon gets asked to leave the stage; *the show off* - he will do anything and actively gives the hypnotist

permission to command them to do any type of stupid act; *the super-suggestible one* - goes up on stage even when she doesn't want to, these people can't help themselves and will usually be the best trance subjects.

(2) The hypnotist performs a few susceptibility tests to weed out anyone who will not go into trance in the first few minutes or is not co-operating.

(3) Only the best subjects are used and the experienced hypnotist knows who they are.

(4) Those on stage have a vested interest to co-operate and even if not in trance, will still perform their acts as if they were. They don't want to be embarrassed by failing to perform so they pretend to be hypnotised. Besides, why did they get up there in the first place? Perhaps because they are exhibitionists.

(5) Most people on stage will actually go into a light trance state and do as they are commanded willingly, stopping only when their morals are being threatened even if it appears otherwise.

Hypnosis cures cancer / warts / performs miracles

Yes and no. It is not hypnosis but the person's beliefs that make miracles. Sure, miracles do occur and have for millennia but the skilled therapist will encourage the individual's belief structure to do the curing and not the hypnotherapy itself. Most of these so-called miracles happen after many months and many sessions, as well as regular home practice. The other side to the coin is that we rarely hear of the failures of hypnotherapy or of any other therapy. It doesn't pay to advertise our failures, just our successes. The bottom line is: if you want a miracle, then you will have to earn it.

Hypnosis can make a person believe that they have touched a burning match and it will leave a blister

True. It has been documented many times that people in trance can create physical symptoms. This may prove to be the cause of religious stigmata such as the bleeding from the hands, feet, side or forehead, where Jesus was said to have been wounded. The power of belief can create illness and great suffering, or we might chose to change our belief systems and cure our health problems.

Post hypnotic suggestions under hypnosis always work

They don't. If there is any underlying psychological cause of your problem, then suggestions will either only work for a short time or not at all. Psychotherapy is usually required, then the post hypnotic suggestions can be applied. When giving up smoking, many people have underlying psychological problems that constantly jeopardise their treatment. Deeper work is then necessary.

I sometimes use the analogy of painting a wall to explain suggestion. To simply paint over a dirty wall without first cleaning it is like using suggestion without first getting to the cause - the paint will eventually peel and fall off. Rubbing back the old paint and repairing the surface is like using psychotherapy to clean up the cause. Then you can apply suggestions. Suggestion for simple problems with no underlying psychological cause is effective when performed by a skilled therapist.

I believe in the power of hypnosis. I have read everything there is to read about it and I want to try it on my long term problem

This person has extremely high expectations which are unlikely to manifest in the first session. She will no doubt be looking for that magical moment when she falls into a deep hypnotic trance state akin to mystical or spiritual bliss. When it doesn't happen, she becomes disillusioned and will probably not bother returning for her next session. This person needs to read this section thoroughly to understand the limitations of hypnotherapy.

I will not remember a thing when I awake

Not true, most people will remember and hear everything while under hypnosis. The command to forget is rarely used today, it is more beneficial for you to remember so that you can repeat it next session or at home. You can generally hear sounds outside the room but you don't pay any attention to them. When listening to a tape of your session you may hear dogs barking and other noises that you didn't notice while in trance. You can become so absorbed in the experience that you had ignored these sounds. Research has shown that people in a relaxed state, not in trance, were just as capable of forgetting experiences as those in a deep trance state. Hypnotic amnesia is only useful when the person needs to forget something but is rarely used in practice today.

I might tell all my secrets or break wind while under hypnosis

Your critical faculty will prevent any unwanted secrets or noises from emerging.

Hypnosis is akin to magic and I can do all sorts of magical things while in trance

Yes and no. Yes, you can learn to leave your body, view distant or past events and fly like a bird. It is argued that the power of imagination creates this sense of magic. It is certainly possible to do these magical things with your mind and there are many documented instances - I have witnessed them myself.

Hypnosis can do anything

We would all like to believe so but hypnosis is just a tool and a technique for accessing our unconscious. It is here that you can, through dedicated practice, achieve some interesting and often mystical experiences. Every shamanic tradition seeks to train the initiate in deep states of trance. Our western mystical heritage is based on Druidic and shamanic mystical tradition. It just depends what you believe. Hypnosis is not magic, however your beliefs have the potential to create your own magic.

I say my affirmations every day but they don't seem to work very well

Verbal affirmations operate on the auditory level and as such will only be useful if you have a strongly developed auditory channel. Use all your senses with emphasis on the visual, auditory and kinesthetic / feeling modalities whilst in a light trance and you will be more successful.

I can only tell the truth when hypnotised

Not at all, you can certainly tell whopping big 'pork pies'.

All memories recovered under hypnosis must be true

Research has shown time and again that memory can be falsified through suggestion by the therapist or by recalling something other than the real event. Although hypnosis enhances recall there is ample evidence that memory can be just as deficient under hypnosis as it is without.

APPENDIX 2

Common Psychological Defenses

Defence mechanisms are programs that run silently and deeply within your unconscious to protect you from traumatic memories - and your inner dragons. Generally speaking, most of us are completely unaware of our defences. The term 'defence' explains how important they are to your self preservation. When a situation arises that upsets your emotional stability, a defence is initiated to shut it down. This protects you from experiencing unpleasant feelings and thoughts. It is not a cure, it is more a means to band-aid the problem until you are ready to deal with its underlying cause.

Denial - You ignore or reject the real situation when you find it too difficult or painful to accept something: *"I don't mind at all that you are working with your ex-wife!"*

Rationalization - You come up with excuses to justify your decisions: *"I can't focus on this new exercise program. I might injure my shoulder and then I can't play bowls."*

Isolation of affect - You are able to intellectualise but not feel the emotion: *"My friend died in a car crash yesterday. I'm sure I will miss him. What's for dinner tonight?"*

Reaction Formation - You act in the opposite direction to what you really feel. This happens, for instance, when you don't like something but don't know how to cope with the consequences of expressing it:

"Wow, a pencil sharpener. What a thoughtful gift. I just love it. It's just what I needed."

Projection - You dump onto others what you find unacceptable within yourself: *"I think about cheating on you, so you must be cheating on me."*

Displacement - You redirect your feelings onto someone else or some other object. For instance, you hate your workmate but instead of confronting her you take it out on your partner when you get home: *"I can't stand the sight of you!"*

Suppression - You defend against your thoughts or feelings about a situation. You push it down so you don't feel it. This is the only conscious defence mechanism: *"I'll just keep doing what I am doing, I'm sure I will get over it."*

Regression - You revert back to a previous developmental stage rather than confront current reality: *"I can't give up my safe, old pillow. I can't sleep without it."*

Sublimation - You redirect unacceptable feelings or urges so that they are socially acceptable: *"I just got a job in the prison system and you should see all those angry people. I am really going to enjoy working there."*

Defences are how we manage our unconscious urges, instincts and drives. They are how we hold back our inner dragons. It doesn't free them from their prisons and it doesn't heal them. It merely binds them with a ball and chain to stop them running amok and disturbing our life.

APPENDIX 3

About Noel Eastwood and Pluto's Cave

Welcome to Pluto's Cave where be dragons, inner selves and wishing wells.

Noel Eastwood is a retired psychologist who has studied and taught tai chi and taoist meditation, astrology and the tarot for more than 30 years. Pluto's Cave is a metaphor he uses for the hidden world of the unconscious.

Dragons are those invisible yet powerful urges that drive us in predetermined ways. They come from our deep unconscious when we are fearful, angry, sad or uncertain. Dragons can be trained to fly and rejoice in their power, yet few initiates know how to do this.

Inner Selves are parts of our psyche splintered off when bad things happen. These, too, live inside our Cave, our deep Unconscious. They feed our dragons when something triggers unpleasant memories.

Wishing Wells are our treasures, those wondrous potentials that lie hidden deep within. For most, they remain untouched throughout an entire lifetime.

Entering Pluto's Cave is a journey into the unconscious for those who seek to tame their inner dragons.

In ancient mystery schools, the term 'initiate' is often used to describe the seeker of knowledge. Their quest is to find and rescue, support and nurture their own injured inner self. As many issues arise from childhood trauma, initiates realise that the dragon is in fact their fears. They develop strategies to manage the issues that held them back in life and stunted their relationships. The trauma of the past can indeed be healed.

Initiates delve into 'magic wishing wells' of the mind, places of discovery and wonder. They learn meditation techniques that have been practiced for centuries to master their fears and emotions. They dip into these wells to learn more about the meaning of life.

You will learn about these metaphors in Noel's books and his newsletters.

Why not join Noel in your own adventure to heal your soul and uncover your potential?

Subscribe to my weekly newsletter for your 15% discount on all ebooks, audiobooks and video lessons – www.plutoscave.com

NOW AVAILABLE AS AN AUDIOBOOK

Other books by Noel Eastwood"

www.ingramcontent.com/pod-product-compliance
Lightning Source LLC
Chambersburg PA
CBHW071917290426
44110CB00013B/1390